CONCILIUM

Religion in the Seventies

CONCILIUM

Concilium 120 (10/1978): Moral Theology

THE
DEATH PENALTY
AND TORTURE

Edited by

Franz Böckle and
Jacques Pohier

A CROSSROAD BOOK

The Seabury Press · New York

1979
The Seabury Press
815 Second Avenue
New York, N.Y. 10017

Library of Congress Catalog Card Number: 79-83936
ISBN: 0-8164-0410-0
ISBN: 0-8164-2200-1 (pbk.)
Printed in the United States of America

CONTENTS

Part III
Psychological and Social Aspects

Part IV
Documentation

Editorial

TORTURE is something we expect to find only historical accounts of. Officially it has disappeared from legal codes. Torture is forbidden by all relevant international declarations, conventions and agreements. Yet in some sixty countries governments either order or at least tolerate the use of torture. In more than a third of the member States of the UN, torture forms part of the armoury of investigation methods or is used to punish prisoners. The so-called psychological methods and the misuse of drugs are constantly gaining favour in this regard. Therefore the topics chosen for this *Concilium* need no further justification. From the moral theological standpoint, we are not concerned merely with the academic question whether torture has fundamentally to be rejected as unethical. The purpose of this volume is rather to expose the historical and social background of torture and to summon all those of good will to the fight for respect for human rights.

We have decided to treat the question of capital punishment at the same time. Admittedly they are two separate problems, yet they have an inner connection. There is a tendency in legal history to leave cruel executions behind and to 'humanize' capital punishment by the pursuit of technical perfection. Yet the difference between the fires of Smithfield, the gas-chambers of Auschwitz and a painless injection seem, when the psychic situation is taken into account, more quantitative than qualitative. Is the progress of humanization to be measured only in terms of advanced techniques of execution? Surely we must rethink the whole question of the right to decide a man's fate. On the other hand, with the use of isolation torture on terrorists we have witnessed an extension of the notion of torture that goes against the nature of examination of suspects and ideas of due punishment.

The increased demand for more general application or reintroduction of capital punishment is clearly related to the escalation of terror and the use of force in social conflict. In these encounters some radical groups show a tendency to 'democratic deinstitutionalization' of capital punishment by revolutionary people's courts. They allow special squads to carry out executions. Where are the roots of this notion of retribution and revenge? Have the Churches and their theology always spoken loudly enough against the idea of retribution? What possibilities are there for the Churches now in this regard? What is already being done? These are questions we try to look for answers to.

We begin with a critical report by a representative of Amnesty International on the present use of torture. There follow reports on the legality and practice of torture in various countries. Since the major religions (Christianity, Judaism, Islam) play an important part in normative thinking in the relevant countries, a main interest in a theological journal must of course be the attitude of these religions to torture and capital punishment. In the third part of this volume we discuss the socio-pyschological and social aspects of the subjects. We close with a report on the latest ecclesiastical standpoints on capital punishment in Canada and the United States.

FRANZ BÖCKLE
JACQUES POHIER

PART I

The Death Penalty and Torture Now

Herbert Radtke

Torture as an Illegal Means of Control

' "SON of a whore, we'll rape your mother. If you don't talk you won't get out of here alive". Then they threatened that if they couldn't get a confession, they'd drag in my mother and sister and rape them in front of me. The blows were so heavy that I kept losing consciousness, and they'd bring me round by pouring cold water on my head. This went on for 12 days' (Mustafa Oglün, Turkey).[1]

'11 March, morning: during the rounds, just by way of experiment, I complained that I felt ill after taking haloperidol and asked that the dose be reduced. This led to my being prescribed even more aminazine than I was already receiving . . . and from 19 January onwards I have been given two halperidol tablets twice daily, that's four tablets in all (and Kozich [2] assures me that this will go on for a long time). This medicine makes me feel more miserable than I have ever felt before; you no sooner lie down than you want to get up; as soon as you walk a couple of steps, you are longing to sit down, and if you sit down, you want to start walking—but there's nowhere to walk. I'm not the only one who's had this sort of thing happen to him: triftazine (trifluoperazine-stelazine), aminazine and other powerful drugs are used on everyone here and bring the same suffering' (Vladimir Gershuni, USSR).[3]

'I was immediately stripped, laid on a bed and systematically tortured—mainly with the *picana* * for about one and a half hours. On Saturday, 17 July, at about 3:00 P.M., I was taken back to the interroga-

---

*An electric rod which the Argentinian police claim to have invented (translator's note)

3

tion room. For an hour or an hour and a half, the *picana* was applied to the most sensitive parts of my body: testicles, breasts, mouth, etc.; after this, the savage mercenaries subjected me to what they called ''the Asian torture'' which consisted of pitching me into drums of water while hanging onto my legs. They did this four or five times until I lost consciousness. When I came to again, I was tortured for another hour and a half with the *picana,* but this time, three rods were used simultaneously. I must also mention that they injected some substance—possibly poisonous or infectious—into the big toe of my right foot, into my testicles and my right arm and that they pulled out the nails of both my big toes and slit one toe open. After this, they applied the *picana* to all these places' (Carlos Baro, Argentinian doctor, arrested 16.7.76).[4]

These are not voices from the dark ages, but reports of things happening today. These are accusations, levelled not at a few sadistic prison guards, but at responsible governments. They are cries for help, not of a few individuals, but of hundreds, of thousands, every day. Most are unheard. The few published reports occasion suspicion and disbelief, because, for most people, torture is something totally unacceptable; and what is unacceptable simply doesn't happen. That torture is unacceptable is made clear by its prohibition in all the relevant international declarations, agreements and conventions. There is scarcely a legal code in which it is a permitted form of punishment.

All the same, there isn't a country in the world where torture is inconceivable: in more than sixty it is systematically practised by the government, or, at the very least, tolerated.[5]

In 1874, Victor Hugo could say: 'torture has once and for all ceased to exist'. Today, we are compelled to recognize that it is more widespread than ever before. In more than a third of the member states of the United Nations, torture is used either as a method of interrogation or as a means of punishing detainees. Torture knows no ideological frontiers: it is practised in Iran, Iraq, Ethiopia, Uganda, Ghana, Guinea, South Africa, Guatemala, Argentina, Chile, Bolivia, Nicaragua, Indonesia, Bangladesh, Afghanistan, USSR, Morocco, Tunisia, Israel and the People's Republic of Yemen.

THE MECHANIZATION OF TORTURE

Rather than go into the various techniques used by torturers, I shall confine my remarks to two clearly recognizable trends.

1. Torture is becoming increasingly scientific. Alongside physical

brutality and mutilation, the use of sophisticated mechanised equipment is becoming more and more common. A particular cause for concern is the growth of psychological and pharmacological methods of torture.[6] While once doctors present at an interrogation were generally there to prevent the victim's death, today, medical science plays an active rôle in improving the torturer's techniques.

2. Because torture is an international phenomenon, improvements in techniques are quickly passed on by the countries developing them. Experiences are continually exchanged and the training of torturers is conducted on an international basis. Fort Gulick and Fort Sherman, US military bases in the Panama Canal zone, run training schemes in the combatting of guerilla and subversive activity, to which 'guests' from Central- and South-American states are invited. According to a report in the *New York Times,* 170 out of the 30,000 South-American 'graduates' from Fort Gulick, hold office as presidents, ministers, supreme commanders, staff officers or directors of the prison service.[7] On 6 November 1973, scarcely two months after the bloody military coup, the Chilean junta's general, Augusto Pinochet, wrote a letter of thanks to Fort Gulick, in which, among other things, he said: 'We should like to express, on behalf of the Chilean army, our gratitude for the professional training we received, and I add to this my personal and sincere good wishes'.[8] A few words from Shah Reza Pahlevi illustrate both points: 'We must no longer torture people; instead we'll turn to the methods used in some highly-developed countries—psychological methods'.[9] It should be mentioned here, that the Shah's words are quite deliberate lies: brutal physical torture has never ceased to exist in Iran; SAVAK, the intelligence and security organization, answerable only to the Shah, is notorious for its cruelty. Notorious also is the 'hot table' (an electronically heated metal bar or plate to which the victim is strapped) which was developed by SAVAK, and which has, up to now, been used only in Iran.

TRAINING THE TORTURER

What sort of people are the professional torturers? They belong to the lowest ranks of the police force, the army and the prison service, but it is striking too that they often form a kind of élite corps. There are certainly a few psychologically disturbed sadists, but, for the most part, professional torturers are conscientious, rather servile people, content simply to 'do their job'. What turns them into the brutal instruments of state power they become, is an ingenious threefold system, which first creates a favourable climate of opinion and then conditions the torturer to both unquestioning obedience and an acceptance of brutality.

1. The potential victim is first 'dehumanized'. Usually this is achieved through an intensive publicity campaign in which already existing prejudices are manipulated by the authorities and a caricature of the 'enemy' constructed. Often, he is credited with a dangerousness and cruelty that in no way corresponds to the reality. Hitler depicted the Jews as parasites, scroungers and as dangerous viruses; General Pattakos, strong-man of the Greek military junta, proclaimed: 'We don't make distinctions between people and people, but we do between people and animals'. It doesn't make much difference who the enemy is; the caricatures are interchangeable but the intention is always the same. In this way, whole sections of the population suddenly cease to be human beings at all. It happens to religious groups (the 'dissident' Baptists in the Soviet Union, Jehovah's witnesses in Malawi), to ethnic and racial minorities (the Kurds in Iran, Iraq, Syria and Turkey), or even to majorities (the Blacks in Rhodesia and South Africa), to social and political groups (students in Greece, Communists in countless countries, the miners in Bolivia, the supporters of the Congress Party in Nepal). The effectiveness of campaigns of this sort is illustrated by an American soldier who fought in Vietnam: 'It wasn't like they were humans. We were conditioned to believe this was for the good of the nation, the good of our country and anything we did was okay. And when you shot someone you didn't think you were shooting at a human. They were a Gook or a Commie and it was okay'.[10]

'Dehumanizing' the enemy is effective for two reasons: it enables the torturer to 'do his work', for he is no longer compelled to regard his victim as a man like himself and it ensures the authorities a certain amount of public support. For what the torturer is doing is 'all for the good of the people'; he is 'protecting the fatherland from Communist (or revisionist) infiltration'; he is 'defending Christian culture (or ensuring the triumph of the glorious revolution'), or—and this is perhaps a shade nearer the truth—'he is actively bringing about the restoration of law and order'.

2. Conditioning to absolute obedience is an important part of the training of potential torturers. It should be remembered that practically all torturers are recruited from professions which have a rigid hierarchical structure and which cultivate unquestioning obedience. This is confirmed by the findings of Professor Stanley Milgram,[11] who shows very clearly the extent to which authority can influence our behaviour, and whose research findings can perhaps be summed up in the words: 'everyone is a potential torturer'. The first torturers' trial, which took place in Greece in 1975, makes the same point. In his concluding address, the prosecutor said: 'The subordinate ranks were conscripted.

They were not, as some people have tried to pretend, volunteers. After they had had every trace of individuality and humanity crushed out of them at KESA,[12] after their lowest interests had been aroused, after they had been threatened, terrorized and mislead, they were let out like wild animals from their cages and set on their brothers to tear them to pieces. Most of them, not having the strength to resist, followed their orders'.[13] One victim described his impressions: 'There were two categories of ESA * men. To the first belonged those who obeyed orders so as to survive . . . To the second category belonged those who had been specially trained so that fascism had become part of their personalities . . . They are not weird monsters but the results of a system of training'.[14] A member of ESA defended himself: 'I beat prisoners, Mr Chairman, they were my orders and that's what I did. A soldier couldn't do anything else but obey'.[15]

3. The way we have become acclimatized to cruelty—for example, through exposure to violence on television—has sparked off a great deal of controversy and no definite conclusions can be drawn [16] at this stage. But in the context of the methods I have already discussed the point seems fairly clear. The simple fact that torturers are usually recruited from special 'hard training' units, confirms this thesis. Further proof is afforded by the fact that every year in the British Army 250 volunteers take part in a 'torture resistance training' course where five methods of torture are practised on them. It is now known that it is precisely these techniques that are used by the British Army in Northern Ireland. The evidence of one Greek torturer completes the picture: 'It is nothing, Mr Chairman, to give someone five blows when you've had sixty from your comrades'.[17] There is evidence that similar methods are used in numerous armies. This participant's account of a special training scheme for troops and officers in the US Marines, appeared in the West-German political weekly magazine *Der Spiegel:* 'Blaring Vietnamese music can be heard above the roar of MGs. An American soldier crouches in the "Tiger Cage", a tiny crate, measuring 0.5 cubic metres. He has a coffee pot for urinating. He hears the gurgling screams of one of his comrades on the "Water Swing", a loping plank, to which he is tied head-downwards with a cloth covering his mouth while cold water is continuously poured into his face. A doctor is standing by to make sure he doesn't drown!'[18] A report in *Stern,*† fully illustrated with photographs reveals that in Brazil, soldiers taking part in similar 'exercises' are, for days at a time, tied to

---

* ESA = Elliniki Stratiotiki Astynomia.
† A West-German political weekly (translator's note).

trees, 'crucified' or buried in mud-holes, and that they are brutally beaten and forced to beat their comrades.[19]

Besides these three main ways of training torturers, there are cases where other factors are important. Amnesty International reports cite conclusive evidence that pressure is often put on individuals: promotion is hinted at and ambition aroused; material rewards are offered which some soldiers—many of whom come from the poorest sections of society—are unable to resist, and all sorts of similar tricks.

Today, in most countries (in so far as Amnesty has been able to investigate), torture is institutionalized. Special organizations grow up, usually within the police or the army, with euphemistic names such as the Argentinian Department for Political Order or the National Information Committee in Chile. They tend to render themselves independent, to become a State within the State, for, as a rule, they are outside the normal hierarchies of parliamentary control and the system of justice. There are also 'private torture organizations' which recruit their members from the security forces: the 'Grey Wolves' in Turkey, the 'White Hand' in Guatemala, the 'Warriors of Christ the King' in Spain, the 'Anti-Communist Alliance' in Argentina, the 'Revenge Underground Organization' in Iran, are all examples of this. These groups frequently work on 'special missions' and are at least tolerated by the government. The 'Grey Wolves' is part of Turkey's former Vice Premier Alparslan Türkes' National Movement Party.[20] The 'White Hand' was founded by Mario Sandoval Alarcon, today Vice President of Guatemala.[21] Sergio Fleurey, leader of the 'Death Squads' in San Paulo, is also head of the DEIC (Departamento de Investacão Criminal).[22]

Something that is common to all torture organizations is that they develop an individual culture with special rituals and language. This involves names for the torturers' techniques (the 'parrot-perch', 'crown of thorns', 'telephone', 'submarine') and ways of describing the interrogation sessions (the 'spiritual seance' in Brazil, the 'tea-party' in Greece) as well as nicknames for or ways of addressing the torturers (Doctor, the Gentle One). It involves too a definite system according to which the torture must be carried out. Evidently the euphemisms and schematization are what make it possible for the torturer to do his work and to regard his job as 'normal'. 'The atmosphere surrounding the torture operation seems to rely on this kind of perverted irony, an *esprit de corps* which, like bravado in wartime, is necessary to sustain the belief that somewhere a higher authority will take responsibility for the crimes committed in the name of the state'.[23]

THE AIMS OF TORTURE

In the Middle Ages torture was exclusively designed to establish the 'truth' and to corroborate the evidence of witnesses. Today, it is usually regarded as a means of procuring information. But because the value of the evidence acquired in this way is at best dubious (the victims are often too ignorant to help themselves except by 'going along with the system' in the hope of buying a few days or hours of relief) as an argument it is far from convincing. For torture to be justified in this way, the consent of the victim would be necessary. Still more persuasive are the practices of the torturers themselves: a few years ago torture was carefully concealed; victims were not released until the tell-tale signs had disappeared and they were warned that their failure to keep silent might lead to an 'unpleasant death'. But for some time now—and this is worth emphasizing—the regimes that practise torture are no longer concerned publically to explain their crimes: in increasing numbers people simply 'disappear' and their fate is rarely publicized. Since the military coup in Argentina about 15,000 people have vanished.[24] Weeks or months after their disappearance, many were found dead with recognizable signs of having been tortured.

It is now emerging that more and more frequently people with apparently no obvious political affiliations are being arrested. They are dragged into an interrogation centre, brutally tortured and, a few days later released again. The authorities no longer hide the fact that these people are being tortured; the victim is scarcely even interrogated (for the interrogation sessions are little more than depraved orgies of abuse). The torturers are concerned simply to keep their victims guessing where and by whom they are to be tortured.

In Cambodia and Ethiopia 're-education' programmes are being established and incredible brutality is used. The press is full of reports of massacres.[25] In Iran during the first three months of 1978, French lawyers have found that more than 100 people were shot for taking part in a peaceful demonstration.[26]

Such practices can have only one purpose: to spread a climate of terror throughout the whole country so as to deter people from any form of (undesirable) political activity. An additional function of torture is to acquire confessions which can, at a later date, be produced in the courts to secure a conviction. Amnesty International has found evidence of this happening, in, for example, both Morocco and Turkey. The authorities, presumably concerned about their reputation abroad, insist on 'correctly ordered' trials so as to present to the world an appearance of legality. In this context the term 'confession' means simply that the victim of torture has been forced to sign a statement; its contents may in no way correspond to what he actually said; he may also never have read it.

One way of assessing the real purpose of torture is to examine the areas in which it is most frequently used. From this it is clear that the torturers' main aim is to spread a climate of terror. The procuring of information is of only secondary importance (not least because investigation and interrogation techniques have been steadily improving) and, apart from a few exceptional instances, it has little credibility. In recent years there has been a decline in the number of cases of confessions being acquired for use in the courts.

THE POLITICAL BACKGROUND OF TORTURE

The examples discussed above show that torture is not the product of any one political ideology, nor is it confined to any one economic or constitutional system. There must, therefore, be something that is common to all countries practising torture (regardless of the image they present of themselves and the practical effects of this) which enables them to do so. A brief historical digression may be permissible here. When Frederick II, king of Prussia and first absolute monarch, prohibited torture in 1740, he made three exceptions: *lèse majesté,* murder and treason,[27] two of which are relevant to our discussion. Frederick's proviso shows how closely the survival of the State depends upon and is identified with the preservation of valid forms of government. This same chain of reasoning operates even today.

Even in 'Socialist' countries, the official (Socialist Unity) parties consider that they, and only they are able to perceive the true road to peace, justice and prosperity. Anyone who dares to cast doubts on these dogmas or who criticizes the official party line is labelled as 'an enemy of the State' by the party leaders. His or her ideas are classed as a 'danger to the people' and so, in order to protect the people, the dissident must either recant or be removed from society.

In non-Socialist countries, it is less easy to observe the way in which this process works. But some facts are beyond dispute: in the 'classical' torture state, the ruling class excludes the majority (or one or more minorities) from effective political participation and/or there is a very unequal distribution of wealth. Inevitably this gives rise to a situation which the government and/or those who possess the country's wealth, regard as a threat. The following extract is Ralph Giordano's analysis of these developments. 'Torture in the western, in the non-Communist world, is the furious reaction of the rich and powerful to the despairing desire for social and political change of the poor and the powerless.

This is the essence of the conflict. The aggression shown by the poor in the face of the unendurable status quo in Asia, in Africa and in Latin America, provides the pretext for torture. This analysis of economic and political power structures shows that torture is the almost inevitable consequence of mass poverty, so it looks as though it will be with us for a long time yet—particularly as it has powerful supporters and patrons. No regime practising torture has ever been internationally boycotted or made to suffer political or economic repercussions. Quite the reverse: torture states are the most desirable areas for investment. The Brazilian government—like the Congo, Persia and Indonesia—ensures that foreign capitalist investors have unequalled facilities and access to the country's mineral resources, labour force and internal markets. But this kind of co-operation between foreign and domestic big business demands political stability. Torture is, at best, regarded as a necessary evil; more usually it is seen as the guarantee of a satisfactory dividend return'.

When I drew attention to this in my film *Im Jahr der Folter* (*In the Year of Torture*), a certain section of the West German press sneeringly referred to me as a 'left-wing trouble maker' and implied that I had exploited the suffering of torture victims for propaganda purposes. In reply I should like to make two points: firstly, all those who appeared in my film (as well as those who, for lack of time, were unable to) themselves expressed the points I made and indeed considered them of overwhelming importance. Secondly, in support of my thesis that torture is used to ensure a good dividend return, I should like to quote the *Wirtschaftswoche,* which, on 1 February 1974 (according to the *Süddeutscher Zeitung* *) quoted Werner Paul Schmidt, former Director of 'Volkswagen do Brazil', as saying: 'Of course the police and the army torture prisoners to get important information; political subversives are naturally often shot without trial. But an objective assessment of the situation is that firmness is essential if we are going to get on. And we are getting on!' Thus speaks an accomplice—torture is the price of progress! [28]

Torture and repression on grounds of race or religion are relatively rare today. But it is important to distinguish between repression purely on grounds of race or religion, and repression where religious or racial persecution is combined with social, economic or political forces. In the case of religion, the use of torture is rare—but this is not because governments regard torture as reprehensible; it is simply that, being

* West German daily, published in Munich but read throughout Germany, of SPD (Social Democratic Party) sympathies; the *Guardian* is the nearest English equivalent (translator's note).

one of the severest instruments of repression, torture is usually only brought into force when social, economic and political disadvantage has driven the group in question into active opposition.

Torture on grounds of race must be regarded differently. This is because the treatment meted out to victims involves methods which must be placed in the 'grey area' between punishment that is merely 'cruel, inhuman and degrading' and treatment which should officially be classed as torture.

OUR RESPONSIBILITY

Peace is more than the absence of war for it involves the realization of the development of each and every individual within his or her elected social system. This ideal is expressed in the International Declaration of Human Rights, which lays down our entitlement to basic physical necessities (to be adequately fed and housed and to receive medical care), as well as to the essential freedoms of religious practice, free speech and free elections in the area we live in. It sets limits on the extent to which the State can restrict the freedom of the individual and asserts the fundamental principles of equality, the right to life, of freedom and security, of justice and a fair legal system and of freedom from torture. These basic principles were expounded thirty years ago and are recognized by all member States of the United Nations. In practice, however, 117 countries were last year found to have violated the principles laid down in the Universal Declaration of Human Rights. And this is just within the limited number of areas that Amnesty has investigated: people are persecuted for their political views, their race, their religion or their sex; state judicial systems are far from just, torture is used, and the death penalty remains in force.[29]

These violations of human rights prevent the construction of a peaceful society at both national and international levels. Internal peace is continually threatened as citizens have to resort to force to resist the State's infringement of their basic rights. In many countries, conflicts of this sort escalate into violent confrontations and this in turn increases the danger of intervention by 'friendly' countries which have pledged their support.

The only way to break out of this vicious circle is to transform the old, non-binding declarations into legally-binding conventions or treaties. At the same time, a special court should be set up, to which the individual can turn when his or her rights have been violated by the State.[30] It would be a step in the right direction if States accused of infringing human rights, did not regard such criticism as an unwarranted interference in their internal affairs.

These developments at international level must be accompanied by an increased sensitivity to the fate of our fellow men and women. A greater awareness of, and commitment to, the cause of human rights on the part of all of us must become something as natural as the relinquishing of individual privileges in the cause of world peace.

WHAT CAN WE DO?

Everyone, whether working as an individual or as part of a group, can contribute to the realization of this ideal. The abolition of torture is so all-embracing an aim that the possible ways of furthering it are correspondingly diverse.

Start by opposing a blind faith in authority wherever you encounter it. Of course, a certain amount of discipline and obedience are essential in any community but they are far too often exploited—it's so convenient for us to do so.

Oppose all violence however it may be glorified or presented as a good in itself. Violence is never 'good', though it is sometimes unavoidable. Brutality and torture, however, cannot be justified anywhere or at anytime. Each attempt to do so is a crack in the walls raised against torture.

Oppose 'dehumanization': colour, creed, political belief and crime (including torture) are not grounds to regard a person as anything other than fully human. Resist the tendency to lump people together and to make crude generalizations, for this is the first step along the road to disaster.

Support the work of the United Nations and other bodies working for international co-operation. Support, too, the idea that real peace demands sacrifices.

Support the victims of torture whenever you learn about them. Play an active part in bringing reports of torture to the attention of a wider public. Protest to the authorities responsible. Send material help to the relatives of the victims of torture.

'Torture must become as unthinkable as slavery'. With these words Sean MacBride launched Amnesty International's 'Campaign for the Abolition of Torture'. But Amnesty cannot achieve this ideal without our support. All men of good will are called to play their part.*

Translated by Miranda Chayton

---

* Amnesty International (from whom all English-language publications cited in the notes are obtainable) can be contacted at: Tower House, 8/14 Southampton Street, London WC2 (translator's note).

Notes

1. Amnesty International, *Türkei-Politische Verfolgung, Folter, Mord* (May, 1977).

2. Evgeny Vladimirovich Kozich, head physician at Oryol Special Psychiatric Hospital.

3. Amnesty International, *Prisoners of Conscience in the USSR*.

4. Amnesty International, *Report of an Amnesty International Mission to Argentina*.

5. Amnesty International, *Annual Report 1976–77*.

6. See also Gustav Keller, *Die Psychologie der Folter* (März, 1978), pp. 39–46.

7. See also Peter Koch and Reimar Ottmanns, *Die Würde des Menschen* (Hamburg, 1977), p. 77.

8. Ibid., p. 80.

9. Cited in 'Torture as State Policy', *Time,* August 16, 1976, reprinted by Amnesty International.

10. *Vietnam Veterans against War,* cited in Amnesty International, *Report on Torture* (London, 1975), p. 65.

11. See also Stanley Milgram, *Obedience to Authority, an Experimental View* (London, 1974).

12. KESA = Kentron Ekeiderseos Stratiotikis Astynomias, the training centre for ESA military police.

13. Amnesty International, *Torture in Greece: the First Torturers' Trial 1975,* p. 36.

14. Ibid., p. 37.

15. Ibid., p. 38.

16. See also *Der Spiegel,* no 51 (1977), pp. 46-60.

17. Amnesty International, *Torture in Greece: the First Torturers' Trial 1975,* p. 38.

18. *Der Spiegel,* no 17 (1976), pp. 126 and 129.

19. See also *Stern,* no 30 (13.9.1970).

20. See also Amnesty International, *Türkei-Politische Verfolgung, Folter, Mord* (May, 1977).

21. See also Amnesty International, *Briefing Paper on Guatemala* (1976).

22. See also, Helio Pereira Bicudo, *Die Todesschwadron unter Anklage* (Mettingen, 1977).

23. Amnesty International, *Report on Torture* (London, 1975), p. 66.

24. Amnesty International, *Report of an Amnesty International Mission to Argentina*.

25. See also *Der Spiegel,* no 15 (1978), pp. 150–54; *Frankfurter Allgemeine Zeitung* (25.3.78).

26. *Le Monde* (8.13.78).

27. Heinz Holzhauer, *Rechtsgeschichte der Folter:* Amnesty International, *Folter-Stellungnahmen, Analysen, Vorschläge zur Abschaffung* (Baden-Baden, 1976).

28. Ralph Giordano, 'Internationale der Einäugigen', *Christ und Welt*, no 42 (1974).

29. Amnesty International, *Annual Report 1976/77*.

30. Otto Trifterer, *Das Folterverbot im nationalen und internationalen Recht — Anspruch und Wirklichkeit:* Amnesty International, *Folter-Stellungnahmen, Analysen, Vorschläge zur Abschaffung* (Baden-Baden, 1976).

François Colcombet

The Country with the Guillotine

THE history of the death penalty in France is full of paradoxes. Though receptive to the ideas of Beccaria, it was also the home of Voltaire, and capital punishment was not abolished there by the revolutionaries of 1789, or later. They merely modernized executions. The guillotine has worked hard since its introduction in 1792.

Throughout the nineteenth century, abolitionists wrote and spoke, often very persuasively. Take Victor Hugo's *Derniers jours d'un condamné à mort* which was, by the end of the century, being consulted the world over: in Italy, for instance, when a statue was erected to Beccaria in 1875 ('once the statue is in place no scaffold could appear without its sinking back into the ground'); in Geneva, when the death penalty was abolished in 1862 ('When will readers of the Bible understand why Cain was not struck dead?'). But the French Republic, though it re-opened the Panthéon to honour Hugo's remains, still remained faithful to the guillotine.

However the number of executions was diminishing markedly: it fell from 161 in 1825 to 12 in 1875, 4 in 1905, 12 in 1930. There was the same tendency in most western countries, and in most of them it has continued since then. After the Second World War, nearly all of western Europe—including Salazar's Portugal—abolished capital punishment. Only Belgium, Spain and France have kept it, and in Belgium it is almost never used, while Spain is on the point of coming into line with the rest of Europe.

The home of the Declaration of the Rights of Man will then be the last bastion of capital punishment, despite the disapproval of its neighbours. Some, like Denmark and Holland, even hesitate to allow the extradition of criminals to France, for fear that they would be executed.

No one has up to now been able to explain this astonishing anachronism. The most that can be said is that France, since the war, has had unique problems. While other countries could set about reconstructing their economies and restoring civil liberties, France was caught up in the enormous difficulties involved in de-colonization. The abolition of capital punishment seemed a secondary problem, if not a complete anomaly, at a time when a seriously threatened government was not merely using the whole legal panoply of repression against its opponents—including the death penalty—but was actually defending itself by establishing State terrorism (arbitrary arrests, torture, summary executions, the use of common criminals for undercover police work, and so on).

General de Gaulle did in fact use his prerogative of mercy quite often (191 political prisoners were reprieved in 1959); and though Bernard Thiry who attempted to assassinate him was executed, Jouhaud and Canal were spared.

With the restoration of peace, the government worked both to catch up economically and to restore civil liberties in an effort to prevent further repercussions from the Algerian war. The death penalty came to be used less and less (from 1961 to 1969 there were only 8 executions for criminal offences). Every indication was that it would soon fall into disuse.

But no. After the events of May 1968, which profoundly shook the whole country, there was a powerful conservative reaction, followed by a distinct tightening-up. There could be no question now of further liberal advance, at least for the moment. Quite the reverse: the accent was put (especially by the then Minister of the Interior, M. Marcellin) on extending the police force and its powers, and generally reinforcing repression. As far as capital punishment was concerned, the situation remained unchanged: between 1969 and 1974, Pompidou used his prerogative of mercy twelve times, and three people were executed.

Meanwhile, the abolitionist movement was gaining support. In 1972 the Communist and Socialist Parties published a common manifesto in which they promised, if returned to power, to abolish the death penalty. The Radical Left Party also subscribed to this manifesto shortly afterwards.

The idea was gaining ground in the governing party too: M. Claudius Petit, a former minister, had long been campaigning vigorously for abolition. The most notable event was the press conference of 11 April 1974, at which Giscard d'Estaing, then standing for the Presidency, declared that he felt 'naturally, like everyone else, a profound distaste for capital punishment'.

It might have been expected that, once in office, the new President, who sought to demonstrate that there was widespread agreement on social reforms, and who had won the support of the Left for lowering the age of majority and for abortion on demand, would do the same for abolishing the death penalty. But this hope has remained unrealized. On the contrary, a self-styled 'Campaign for the Safety of the French people' gradually developed, instigated by none other than the Minister of the Interior, M. Poniatovski, which was to have a major influence on public opinion.

Whether or not there has been a sharp rise in crime it is impossible to say. The arguments and statistics of both the government and its opponents are equally suspect. But instead of trying to reassure people worried by the eager dramatization of spectacular crimes by certain newspaper and television reporters, the Minister used public concern as a pretext for demanding tougher repression, and closer supervision of those sections of the population believed to be dangerous. There was certainly no question now of abolishing capital punishment.

In January 1976 this campaign reached its climax—over the Patrick Henry affair. Henry had kidnapped and murdered a child, in peculiarly unpleasant circumstances. When he was arrested, the partisans of capital punishment had a field day. Not only did the Minister of the Interior lend his support by letting it be known that he hoped Henry would be condemned to die, but—an unprecedented event—the Minister of Justice publicly expressed the same opinion. These indiscretions finally backfired on their authors. Patrick Henry was saved, following the brilliantly-conducted defence by Maître Badinter. First Poniatovski and then Lecanuet were removed from office after several draft bills relating to 'the safety of the French people' failed to get through Parliament. One in particular, on the right to search vehicles, though passed by both houses, was declared unconstitutional.

The new Minister of Justice was M. Peyrefitte, long known as an opponent of capital punishment, who had chaired the Committee on Violence set up on 20 April 1976. The committee's final report, published under the title, 'An Answer to Violence', concluded with a series of recommendations, one of which was the abolition of the death penalty (to be replaced by preventive detention in serious cases).

Despite this recommendation, despite the President's 'profound distaste' for capital punishment, the government has not yet made any attempt to get Parliament to abolish it. Peyrefitte explained his position in an article in *Le Monde* on 25 August 1977. In it he presented the essence of the abolitionist case—that the death penalty was incompatible with liberal humanism: 'Anyone with humanist ideals will hesitate at the prospect of putting another human being to death in cold blood'. It also undermined the State's authority: 'How can it demand people's support against violence while setting such an example of supreme legal violence?' Peyrefitte even went so far as to say 'that it is as criminal for a judge to condemn a criminal to death as for a criminal to commit a crime'—strong words from the pen of a Minister of Justice! Finally, he admitted that the death penalty could not undo the crime, nor was it a deterrent. His conclusion, however, was not what one would have expected: 'prudence' and 'realism', he said, dictated that one should not move too fast, but he had 'the firm hope that, when the time is ripe, a humanitarian solution will be found for the problem without antagonizing public opinion'.

In this he was being no more than realistic: many people—a great many, to judge by the opinion polls—are against abolishing capital punishment. We hear very little from them—but after all, they have the law on their side. Far more of the French want to keep the guillotine than are actually members of either the National League against Crime and for the Death Penalty or the 'Legitimate Defence Committee' led by a retired former president of the State Security Court. And even though the only politicians who support them publicly belong to the Right or the Extreme Right, it seems virtually certain that many left-wing voters see no need to abolish capital punishment—despite the official stance of the parties subscribing to the common manifesto.

This tacit resistance paralyzes the abolitionists, who in any case go in more for sound and fury than for serious efforts at persuasion.

One may add a postscript to this gloomy picture: the terrorism now taking place in Germany, Ireland, Italy, and, to a lesser degree, in France, has produced an unexpected backlash in our country. When, at the end of 1977, a socialist Deputy suggested inserting a proposal to abolish the death penalty in a text on civil liberties then being debated in Parliament, M. Foyer, a former Minister of Justice, declared that such a proposal would be 'totally inopportune' at a time when 'a peculiarly virulent international terrorism' was on the increase.

Thus, over the years, though the abolition of the death penalty has been more or less on the agenda in France, it remains, for the foreseeable future, 'inopportune'.

Translated by Rosemary Sheed

Alberto Iniesta

The Death Penalty: Legislation and Practice in Spain

I WENT downstairs in the usual way to collect the newspaper and when I went back to the kitchen where my companions—Assumptionist priests with whom I live on a parish mission—were preparing breakfast, I told them with a horrified look, pointing to the paper: '65 people killed in a terrorist attack!' They were appalled; then I added smiling: 'No, they are just those killed on the roads this weekend'. 'Ah, that's all right!' they said with relief. Then they realized my ploy. It made us realize that in most countries—the figure here refers only to Spain—we pay a high tribute of human lives in traffic accidents, which strikes us as unfortunate but inevitable and 'normal', without thinking that society is about to collapse, but deaths in terrorist attacks, which do not amount to even 2% of those killed in traffic accidents, make us extremely nervous, even hysterical. This reveals a series of collective mechanisms which we need to unmask if we are to approach the problem in a calm, civilized, human, and, above all, Christian way.

It is true that terrorists take life consciously, voluntarily and unjustly and that they usually attack those who by their special eminence or function as guardians of the public order, are most in a position to influence society. This means that our judgment on these terrorist attacks cannot be other than absolute condemnation and rejection without any form of palliative, but for the common good of society, we must put their effects into proportion and not play the terrorist's own game by meeting terror with terror, savage violence with savage violence. This would bring two evils to society each of which, in my view, is more serious than the possible death of individuals. The first is that society would forget the precious, hard-won treasure represented by respect for the human person, for justice, for the law and for equanimity by placing itself on the same moral level as the terrorists, acting equally cruelly and out of proportion. The second is that governments would come to adopt such measures of vigilance and repression, affecting all citizens, as preventive measures that we would virtually all come to be treated as presumed terrorists, thereby eliminating or at least diminishing a whole series of basic freedoms and rights inseparable from modern human dignity.

I state this at the outset of this article because in the situation in which many countries find themselves at the present, terrorized by terrorism, it is not only possible for governments to lose their democratic nerve and take dictatorial decisions, but even for the Church itself to become infected with this compulsive desire for security and order at any price and stimulate or at least legitimize the 'secular arm' to take the energetic measures that some seem to wish. If this happens, not only would countries moving towards democracy remain very far from the ideal, but those that have achieved it some time ago would suffer an unfortunate process of regression.

Having said this, I propose to give some facts on the present situation regarding the death penalty in Spain and then, in the third part, to make a short personal judgment on the situation, ending by expressing a wish for the Church to be an agent of humanization and progress in this matter, declaring itself unequivocally against the death penalty.

THE DEATH PENALTY IN SPAIN
FROM THE NINETEENTH CENTURY TO THE PRESENT

1. From the Gallows to the Garrote

Ferdinand VII, at the beginning of the nineteenth century, substituted the traditional method of the gallows by that of the garrote in an attempt to reconcile 'the necessary rigour of justice with humanity' and also to avoid the infamous character of the gallows. The garrote has since then remained the usual system in Spain except for offences against the Code of Military Justice. It is notable that in fact the garrote has taken on the same infamous character in popular imagination as is shown by its usual name of 'Garrote Vil.'

2. A Short Period of Abolition and Reinstitution

The Second Republic has the honour of having suppressed the death penalty in Spain in 1932, although in 1934, with the two-year swing to the right, it was reintroduced into the Code for certain acts of terrorism. Franco re-established it with no limitation on 5 July 1938, 'as being what is proper to a strong and justice-dealing State' as is said in the preamble to the law—one of those 'which require neither explanation nor justification because it is imposed and dictated by reality itself'.

3. Most Recent Executions

As is well known, Franco intervened in a very personal way in the application of the final penalty which was applied with enormous frequency in the years of the Civil War and those immediately following. This was not the case in the last decades of Franco rule. Since 1963, the following have been executed: Julián Grimall of the Communist Party in 1963; Pedro Martínez, a soldier accused of robbery with homicide in 1972; Salvador Puig Antich, anarchist; and Hein Chez, a Polish subject, in 1974; Angel Otaegin and Juan Prades of ETA; José Humberto Baena, Ramón García Sanz and José Luis Sánchez Bravo of FRAP in September 1975, an execution which caused a great stir both in Spain and in the world at large. I know this to my cost as I published a homily on the following 4th October which obliged me to spend a few weeks outside Spain in Rome, on the advice of the Cardinal Archbishop of Madrid, in the face of various threats and pressures from the Government and the Far Right.

4. The Association for the Abolition of the Death Penalty

AAPM began its work in 1976, bringing together a group of people from all over Spain who had always been prominent abolitionists: Carande, the present President; García Valdés, the Vice-President and at present Director of Penitential Institutions; María Asunción Salinas, the Secretary; and others like Aranguren, Gimbernat, the writer of this article, etc. On 4 March 1977, AAPM made its existence publicly known by holding a round table conference in the Atheneum of Madrid during which various speakers studied the death penalty from different points of view: historical, juridical, sociological, anthropological, theological and ethical. Besides this it has made regular contact with leading figures in the Church, the Government and the Judiciary, both civil and military, and has also made contact with similar associations in France, Italy and other countries.

5. *The Road to Abolition*

On 28 December 1977, the Senate rejected by a margin of 12 votes a proposed law to abolish the death penalty, introduced by Villar Arregai, an independent socialist. In May 1968 (when this article was written) there was a partly abolitionist law projected which was due to come before Parliament for approval, which it is hoped will be obtained. In this proposal the death penalty would disappear from the Civil Code, being replaced by forty years imprisonment, which would never be reduced to less than 20. The death penalty would remain in the Code of Military Justice and would be applied even to civilians who caused the death of a soldier or a member of the Forces of Public Order if they were militarized at the time. It is worth noting that in January 1977 acts of terrorism had been moved to the Civil Penal Code which means that these crimes would not be punishable by death except if the victims belonged to the army. The whole proposal can be seen as a good step forward, though incomplete. This is the view of García Valdés and Gimbernat although the latter considers the number of years of imprisonment excessive since in nearly all the countries of Western Europe, this varies between 10 and 15 years, but this also has to be seen in relation to the reform of the Civil Code which is at present being undertaken.[1]

6. *And Christians?*

Naturally, AAPM and other abolitionist groups count Christians among their members, but I would like to look briefly at whether Christian confession influences an abolitionist attitude in Spain. I have to confess that the overall view is somewhat disappointing. For one thing, the episcopate as a whole has not made its views known either way, either for or against the death penalty. During the full session of the Bishops' Conference held in December 1977, when a document on the present-day political situation was being prepared, I introduced a motion for this to include a petition for the death penalty to be suppressed, but my proposal was not accepted. Personally some bishops are abolitionist while others waiver and abstain.

With regard to politicians, remember that it was precisely the Second Republic, regarded as atheist or agnostic and anti-clerical, which abolished the death penalty, while it was at least partly reintroduced during the swing to the right which was overtly Christian in character. Later, Franco, whose claims to Catholicism and religious practices were well known to all, as were his close links with the Spanish Church during so many years, not only re-established the penalty with apparent joy and conviction, but carried it out with appalling frequency.

Finally, to complete this equivocal picture we have at present the evidence that the stance taken by the main parties on the subject once more proves the sad fact that Christians are either less abolitionist or indifferent, while those known as atheists or agnostics are decidedly abolitionist. So the Popular Alliance and the Centre Democratic Union, far right and centre right respectively, did not include abolition in their programmes when the Constitution was being drafted while the PSOE (Socialist), the PSP (Independent Socialist), before it joined the PSOE, and the PCE (Communist) have been and are firmly abolitionist. This surely is a lamentable state of affairs which should give us pause for thought.

A VALUE JUDGMENT ON THE DEATH PENALTY

Although in the space available it is not possible to present a full series of arguments against the death penalty—which are probably studied more directly in other articles in this issue—I would not like to stop without expressing my own thoughts on the matter as concisely as possible.

1. The Death Penalty Is Useless

Statistics demonstrate that its retention or suppression has no effect on the numbers of crimes committed. Furthermore, the death of the offender neither benefits anyone nor restores anything. Remember the argument of the wife of Teqoa before David.

2. It Is Immoral

That is it demoralizes, it gives a bad example. The criminal may be a pervert, mentally disturbed or disturbed in some other way, but society is on principle calm, serene and reasonable with well-thought-out laws and a body of well-balanced persons of high moral stature to apply these laws. It is monstrous for it to place itself on the same level as a criminal out of sheer vengeance. Furthermore, there is always the possibility of an error of judgment, which is totally irreparable.

3 It Is Unnecessary

For the defence of society it is enough to shut the offender away, and this only for the time necessary to reform him through means of proper treatment, never seeing prison as a means of humiliation and vengeance.

4. *It Is Pessimistic*

It refuses to believe that we possess means of helping a man to a complete regeneration or at least to an improvement or, at the very least, to attempt to improve. The death penalty seeks a clear-cut solution, rooting out evil through the execution of the offender—as if one evil could ever abolish another. It forgets that the death penalty is demonstrably productive of crime and that only by curing the delinquent can the evil really be eliminated.

5. *It Is Unjust*

A competitive and consumer society, which *teaches* its members to struggle for success at any price, engenders violence; a society structurally based on so many injustices breeds delinquency, then refuses to recognize its own fruits but seeks to eliminate them from its bosom through a false puritanism making its weakest members scapegoats for sins which belong largely to society as a whole.

6. *It Is Anti-Christian*

Even though the Bible, for situational reasons that are always external to the thought of God, deals largely with violence and death, the general orientation of Revelation even in the Old Testament is clearly in favour of life, forgiveness and hope. God prevents the murderer Cain from being executed in his turn. The law of the Talion is clearly designed to set limits in order to avoid excesses of vengeance. God is the origin of life and therefore all life is sacred, even animal life. Man is the image of God and does not lose this image even when he sins. In the New Testament, Jesus of Nazareth clearly promulgates his law of love, even love for one's enemies, and of forgiveness without limit up to seventy times seven. This means forgiveness even at the cost of one's own life, as he himself died on the cross forgiving his enemies from his heart. This is not something extra, it is the basic law of Christianity and it is to be applied not only to the conduct of the individual but to that of society.

THE 'HOURS' OF GOD

The Church has received from the risen Lord and from his Spirit a treasure whose riches are not completely understood, nor can they always be applied immediately. This treasure is like that of the Scribe who continued to draw old and new things from it. So the Church at the beginning was unable to draw, from the concept of man as the Son of God, consequences that would prevent slavery, the exploitation of man by man, torture, etc. The Church first ignored these, then tolerated them, then practised them, and has lately come to condemn them as incompatible with its evangelical principles. So it could be now—now that we have a society seeking greater justice and brotherhood—that the Church receives one of these 'signs of God' and comes to realize that the death penalty runs contrary to the teaching of Jesus, which is fundamentally a lesson of love, forgiveness and hope.

For this reason I believe that all Christians should reflect on this subject together, as is being done in this issue of *Concilium,* and publicly express our choice for life, demanding not only the abolition of the death penalty where it still exists, but declaring that today, in our historical and cultural context, we consider this penalty contrary to Christian thought. In this way we would contribute to offering our society criteria that would help to strengthen attitudes of serenity, magnanimity and humanity, which are always very necessary, but especially so in these times of cultural crisis. This would help to overcome reactionary temptations and to stimulate efforts at searching, growing and moving forward.

Translated by Paul Burns

Note

On 6 July 1978, two months after I wrote this article, the full session of the Congress of Deputies approved the abolition of the death penalty in the forthcoming Constitution with the proviso I have already indicated concerning military jurisdiction. The proposal, whose formulation stemmed from the UCD (Centre-Right) was approved by the whole spectrum of political shades from the Centre-Right to the Left with 15 members of the Popular Alliance (Extreme Right) abstaining and a few isolated votes against. At the present moment (mid-August) the Senate is debating the draft of the Constitution.

James F. Bresnahan

Death as a Penalty in the United States of America

IN THE decade 1967–1977, death as a penalty was in abeyance throughout the United States. The last two executions occurred in 1967, one in California, the other in Colorado. Then, in 1977, the bizarre case of Gary Gilmore, culminating in his execution by firing squad in Utah, ended the period of moratorium. Although no other death sentences have been executed, it is possible that a new spate of executions will now follow Gilmore's. On the other hand, the history of this period does not make that certain. For, although there are many persons, convicted of crime and sentenced to death, who await execution in various state prisons around the United States, and although there exists a strong groundswell of public opinion favoring the passage of laws which *permit* the imposition of the death penalty, it is *not* at all clear that popular opinion actually *favors* execution of these death sentences. Nor is it clear that many public officials are really eager to see that executions are carried out.

A strange and puzzling struggle has developed between opponents of the death penalty and the many people who are concerned that violent crime, especially 'street crime' threatening ordinary folk in urban areas, should be vigorously sanctioned. This struggle and its implications seem destined to be fully understood only by historians in the future, not by contemporary participants in this history. What can be fruitfully discussed now is the *legal status* of the death penalty as of 1978 in the United States. For the courts are the forum in which the

27

most publicized and influential discussion of the death penalty has
taken place.

CONSTITUTIONALITY OF THE DEATH PENALTY IN CALIFORNIA, 1972

During the ten years prior to 1967, fewer executions were carried out
in the United States in each year. By 1967, significant discussion
seemed to focus primarily on the possibility that death as a punishment
might be finally excluded *not* by legislative action but by *judicial interpretation* of constitutional provisions (whether of state constitutions
or of the Federal Constitution).[1]

The first such case dealing with the issue of constitutional validity
was decided in California in 1972. It involved interpretation only of that
state's constitution by the California Supreme Court, thus was limited
in its jurisdictional impact to California. By a vote of six to one, that
court in *People v. Anderson* [2] held that the death penalty was now to be
considered both 'cruel' and 'unusual', thus constitutionally forbidden
by Article I, Section 6 of the California constitution.

Already, however, a counter trend of popular anxiety about violent
'crime in the streets' of urban America had begun, and the politically
conservative, former movie actor, Governor of California immediately
initiated a popular referendum to amend the Constitution of that state
so that the decision in *Anderson* would be nullified. This amendment
passed within the year.[3] But, no executions have yet taken place in
California as a result of this amendment.

The reasoning of the California Supreme Court in the *Anderson*
opinion seems to me to suggest one reason for this anomalous situation.

In deciding that case, the California Supreme Court was faced with
strong precedent accepting the death penalty in California—the penalty
had been common at the time of the adoption of the state constitution
in 1849 and subsequently the California Supreme Court had repeatedly
affirmed death sentences, even as recently as 1968 without any sugges-
tion that it might be unconstitutional. How could Article I, Section 6
now be construed to invalidate a continuous practice in California since
1849? Mr Chief Justice Wright, writing the opinion of the majority, first
called attention to the obligation of a common law court to interpret the
provisions of the constitution 'in the light of contemporary standards';
he cited the well known federal precedent *Trop v. Dulles*,[4] to the effect
that, by reason of this kind of constitutional limitation, the power to
punish must be exercised 'within the limits of civilized standards'.
Then he had to identify the proper source for understanding the content
of these contemporary, 'civilized' standards. Here we find a clue to the

continuing widespread disinterest in actually seeing the death penalty executed, a disinterest even amongst some of the persons who advocate the availability of the death sentence in what they interpret to be an increasingly violent society. Chief Justice Wright found the proper source of insight into contemporary 'evolving standards of decency that mark the progress of a maturing society' not in public opinion polls, not in the actual willingness of juries to impose the death penalty, not in the refusal of elected legislators to act to repeal the death sentence statutes, from the criminal code, but in the actual attitude and actions of those public officials who have *direct personal experience* of the death penalty—in what I might characterize as *praxis*.

Although death penalty statutes do remain on the books of many jurisdictions, and public opinion polls show opinion to be divided as to capital punishment as an abstract proposition, the infrequency of its actual application suggests that among those persons called upon to actually impose or carry out the death penalty it is being repudiated with ever increasing frequency. . . . What our society does in actuality belies what it says with regard to its acceptance of capital punishment.[5]

Chief Justice Wright then identified the dehumanizing and brutalizing character of the entire process from conviction to execution as the reason for this refusal to execute on the part of those members of society who have direct experience of the death penalty; and so he concluded that the death penalty must be regarded as both cruel and unusual within the contemporary meaning of the California constitution.

CONSTITUTIONALITY OF THE DEATH PENALTY IN THE ENTIRE UNITED STATES, 1972 TO 1976

Between the decision in *People v. Anderson*, 17 March 1972, and the enactment of the amendment overturning that decision, 7 November 1972, another court decision was rendered which also contributed to the 1967–1977 moratorium on execution of any of the persons in California and elsewhere already sentenced to death. This was the decision of the United States Supreme Court in *Furman v. Georgia*,[6] rendered on 29 June 1972 between the *Anderson* decision and the amendment of the California constitution. By contrast with that California decision, the *Furman* case interpreted the Eighth Amendment of the Constitution of the United States which, through the 'due process' clause of the Fourteenth Amendment, constitutes a restraint upon the legislative power of all of the fifty states.

The *Furman* case effectively prevented executions between 1972 and 1976 because its meaning was ambiguous. It was read to cast doubt on the constitutional validity of the death penalty as such. The case was decided by a five to four majority, and all nine Justices wrote separate opinions. The majority of five decided that the death penalty could not be imposed *in the precise cases before them,* but their individual reasoning in five separate opinions by no means coincided. Two of the Justices, Mr Brennan and Mr Marshall, wrote lengthy opinions taking a decisive position analogous to that taken by the Supreme Court of California in the *Anderson* case. The death penalty as such, they said, is 'cruel and unusual' within the meaning of the Eighth Amendment, thus henceforth to be absolutely forbidden throughout the United States. These two Justices make arguments similar to but more elaborate than that of Mr Chief Justice Wright, and the content of their opinions is theologically relevant.

Mr Justice Brennan's opinion emphasizes the need and basis for a progressive interpretation of the Eighth Amendment of the Constitution:

> A Constitutional provision 'is enacted, it is true, from an experience of evils, but its general language should not, therefore, be necessarily confined to the form that evil had theretofore taken. Time works changes, brings into existence new conditions and purposes. Therefore a principle, to be vital, must be capable of wider application than the mischief which gave it birth'. [7]

Then he affirms: 'the basic concept underlying the [Clause] is nothing less than the dignity of man. . . . The State, even as it punishes, must treat its members with respect for their intrinsic worth as human beings'.[8] Justice Brennan deals with these phrases legally, not theologically, by identifying the components of the constitutional test to be applied. Is a punishment (1) degrading, (2) arbitrarily imposed, (3) unacceptable by contemporary standards, and (4) excessive because pointless? For Justice Brennan, a convergence of these defects in death as a punishment justifies the Court in proscribing it.

A significant moment in this argument occurs when Mr Justice Brennan notes, as did the California Supreme Court, that the death penalty is inflicted with increasing rarity; he deduces from this that death is being inflicted *arbitrarily* on but a few of the many convicted persons who equally deserve execution under the laws of the various states. And, in considering whether the death penalty with all its perceived cruelty might be justified by the principle of utility—as a deterrent— Brennan points out that death can deter only if it is invariably and swiftly imposed; but the very reluctance of American society to see death inflicted frequently and without the delay required to be certain of its justice makes this now and henceforth impossible. And this reluctance reflects a public conviction which Brennan interprets to be moral: ' . . . if the deliberate extinguishment of human life has any effect at all, it more likely tends to lower our respect for life and brutalize our values'.[9] Again, then, an appeal to what might be called *praxis* is at the heart of the legal argument.

Mr Justice Marshall structures his argument from the same developmental principle found in the Brennan opinion and in *People v. Anderson:* it is from 'evolving standards of decency that mark the progress of a maturing society' that an interpretation of the Eighth and Fourteenth Amendments must be derived. His argument develops differently from Brennan's chiefly in emphasizing the history of the movement for abolition of death as a penalty and in asking, finally: 'The question now to be faced is whether American society has reached a point where abolition is not dependent on a successful grass roots movement in particular jurisdictions, but is demanded by the Eighth Amendment'.[10] Justice Marshall then examines reasons why a legislature might claim it reasonably substitutes death as a penalty for imprisonment—he asks, therefore, whether it is reasonable to employ this severe a penalty, or is it at this point in history *unnecessary* cruelty? Thus, Marshall implicitly places the *burden of proof* on anyone who would advocate the continued constitutional validity of capital punishment! In this he seems to go farther than Brennan, and certainly well beyond the basic stance of the other three Justices (Douglas, Stewart, and White) who voted in the majority of five to find the death penalty in these cases unconstitutional. Marshall examines six purposes that might be alleged by legislatures to justify death as a penalty—retribution, deterrence, prevention of repetitive crimes, encouragement of guilty pleas and confessions, eugenics, and economic utility (i.e., a cheaper punishment). He concludes that neither individually nor together do these purposes supply sufficient justification of a punishment whose cruelty now is generally perceived.

In the most moving part of his opinion, Justice Marshall argues that not only is capital punishment an irrational measure for any legislature today, thus unconstitutionally cruel, but that it is now 'morally unacceptable to the people of the United States' and on that grounds, too, unconstitutionally violates the Eighth Amendment. As in the *Anderson* opinion and Mr Brennan's opinion in this case, Justice Marshall's problem is how to establish this as 'fact'. Is it simply a matter of consulting empirical studies of public opinion? Marshall urges the need to base this judgment about popular moral conviction on the reaction of an '*informed* citizenry'.[11] The fewer the number of executions and the more 'private' due to a generations-old custom of not having public executions, the more serious becomes the problem of informing the citizenry. Marshall thus faces directly the issue whether public desire for retribution against burgeoning violent crime is a factor which can justify continued use of death as a penalty, or whether this is a factor which ultimately must be discounted in assessing the moral judgment of the citizenry about death as a penalty. Marshall's answer is important for a theological examination of the *human* meaning of death as a penalty:

> I cannot believe that at this state in our history, the American people would ever knowingly support purposeless vengeance. Thus, I believe that the great mass of citizens would conclude on the basis of the material already considered that the death penalty is immoral and therefore unconstitutional.[12]

Justice Marshall then calls attention to the discrimination against deprived racial and ethnic minorities involved in the imposition of death. He thereby suggests the link between the death penalty and the whole history of the 'capital' punishment of slavery and that racist segregation and discrimination deriving from racial slavery. He concludes: 'Assuming knowledge of all the facts presently available regarding capital punishment, the average citizen would, in my opinion find it shocking to his conscience and sense of justice'. Justice Marshall continues:

> At a time in our history when the streets of the Nation's cities inspire fear and despair, rather than pride and hope, it is difficult to maintain objectivity and concern for our fellow citizens. But, the measure of a country's greatness is its ability to retain compassion in time of crisis. No nation in the recorded history of man has a greater tradition of revering justice and fair treatment for all its citizens in time of turmoil, confusion, and tension than ours. This is a country which stands tallest in troubled times, a country that clings to fundamental principles, cherishes its constitutional heritage, and rejects simple solutions that compromise the values which lie at the roots of our democratic system. . . . Only in a free society could right triumph in difficult times, could civilization record its magnificent advancement. In recognizing the humanity of our fellow beings we pay ourselves the highest tribute. We achieve a major milestone in the long road up from barbarism and join the approximately 70 other jurisdictions in the world which celebrate their regard for civilization and humanity by shunning capital punishment.'[13]

Here we find an appeal directly to the constitutional idealism which underlies the practical reluctance of public officials to execute, and a claim that this idealism is in fact widely shared.

In spite of these arguments in the Brennan and Marshall opinions, their three colleagues in the majority limited the decision in *Furman* to proposed executions where *arbitrary and capricious imposition* of the penalty violates due process of law—thus is also 'cruel and unusual', in the words of Mr Justice Stewart,

> In the same way that being struck by lightning is cruel and unusual. For, of all the people convicted of rapes and murders in 1967 and 1968, many just as reprehensible as these, the petitioners are among a capriciously selected random handful upon whom the sentence of death has in fact been imposed.[14]

Thus, in *Furman* a hint was given by Justices Douglas (who retired subsequently), White, and Stewart, that if legislatures could find a way of avoiding arbitrariness and caprice, the death penalty would *not* be *in itself* 'cruel and unusual'. Their emphasis on *procedural* rather than substantive characteristics of death as a penalty was echoed in the opinions of the four dissenters in the disposition of the *Furman* case, Chief Justice Burger, Justices Blackmun, Powell, and Rehnquist. Many state legislatures, responding to popular fear and anger, enacted new death statutes which sought to meet these standards.

In 1976, the Supreme Court decided another series of death penalty cases based on new statutes providing for various procedures to direct and control the discretion of the jury (usually by enumerating aggravating and mitigating circumstances which would purport to control discretion of juries and judges at *the trial level,* thus strive to eliminate that species of caprice and arbitrary imposition of death as a penalty). By a majority of seven to two (only Brennan and Marshall dissenting) the Court upheld the death sentences in three of these cases: *Gregg v. Georgia, Profitt v. Florida,* and *Jurek v. Texas.* On the other hand, at the same time by a five to four vote the Court also reversed the death sentences in two cases, *Woodson v. North Carolina* and *Roberts v. Louisiana;* three justices (Stewart, Powell, and Stevens, who replaced Douglas) found insufficient protection against caprice in the statutes involved and were joined by Brennan and Marshall, while the four justices who originally dissented in *Furman* again dissented here.[15] It was subsequent to these decisions that Gary Gilmore was executed under a Utah statute similar to those involved in the *Gregg, Profitt* and *Jurek* cases. There now seems little probability that the view of Justices Brennan and Marshall will persuade their present colleagues on the Supreme Court.[16]

THEOLOGICAL REFLECTIONS

The public character of the argument in these common law constitutional decisions makes them a significant source for understanding the problems involved in developing a theological analysis of the human experience of the death penalty and in theorizing about it as a social issue. The fate of Justices Brennan's and Marshall's arguments suggests a lesson for theologians and for planners of pastoral practice. As I see it, the continuing effort of many church folk (including the Roman Catholic Bishops of the United States) to bring about elimination of the death penalty from public life will depend for its success upon *informed* 'experience' of the largest number of the citizens. Abstract argument alone has not effectively communicated the basic human values at stake as these have been grasped in the experience of the few public officials directly concerned with executions. The actual infliction of death has long since been hidden from sight of all but select public officials and witnesses who are present in the 'death house'. The bizarre, irrational story of the execution of Gary Gilmore in Utah in 1976 does not seem by itself to have provided an experience of the meaning of the death penalty sufficiently vivid to provoke a popular renewed campaign for legislative abolition; on the other hand neither does it seem to have stimulated strong desire amongst ordinary people to hear more reports of actual executions. Ambivalence prevails. Unscrupulous politicians have a stake in exploiting *un*informed public opinion while conscientious legislators are threatened with loss of election for being 'permissive' and 'soft on crime' if they do not join in the enactment of death penalty statutes. Faced with this kind of situation, the incumbent Governor of New York has vetoed a death penalty statute and promised to commute all death sentences imposed if the statute is subsequently passed over his veto by the legislature of that state. But, shortly before this, the incumbent mayor of New York City (who in fact has no legislative or executive duties with the death penalty) appears to have achieved his election in part by advocating the renewed execution of violent criminals. In these circumstances new strategies based on new forms of argument and persuasion are called for from Christians who abhor the use of death as a penalty.

It would seem to me, therefore, that the problem of the death penalty can be dealt with adequately only when Christian theologians take the hint of Mr Justice Marshall, connect this problem of death penalty with that of slavery and racism, perceive the possibility of 'development of doctrine' in the former as in the latter, and then make a careful argument about the symbolic and 'sacramental' impact within contemporary civilization of state action which causes death. The argument must, above all, be linked to *positive* actions which cherish life, especially the life of the powerless and oppressed.

This combination of argument and practice can, I believe, confront a popular fear of violence which leads ordinary people to reaffirm a kind of common sense conviction that the State must, in the abstract 'essential' order, have the *right* to inflict death as a penalty. Argument, therefore, based on practice, must emphasize the *historical* perception that such a 'right' ought never again be exercised. To inflict death 'officially' in this era of history must be shown to mean an irresponsibly dangerous step backwards toward attitudes of readiness for war and indifference about human oppression. That can only be shown if Christians discover ways to take self-sacrificial risks, risks which demonstrate their conviction that war must not be waged and that oppression must be relieved. Human survival depends on introducing into every dimension of human affairs, at every level, a persistent, active sensitivity to human dignity. Determined efforts to cherish every human life alone can illustrate and bring about more persuasive articulation of effective arguments that death as a penalty must be abandoned and *can be*. Lived compassion and mercy alone will make political argument persuasive.

It seems to me that such a programme must be based on a central belief of Christians, one strangely, and ironically, seldom invoked in discussions of death as a penalty. The Christian religion derives its very existence from the death of a man who was unjustly, indeed arbitrarily and capriciously, hung from the gibbet of the cross! What are the practical implications of this belief in this era of human history, 'after the Holocaust' and wars of historically unparallelled ferocity and cruelty? What expressions of compassionate mercy toward other human beings, *all* other human beings however 'guilty', will be capable of bringing home to Christians, and then perhaps also to those who observe Christian behaviour, that Christ's death if 'believed in' as *praxis* can powerfully transform this world? It is this challenge that I find inextricably linked to our contemporary struggle to eliminate death as a penalty.

Notes

1. See: A. Goldberg and A. Derschowitz, 'Declaring the Death Penalty Un-constitutional', 83 *Harvard Law Review* 1773 (1970).

2. 6 Cal. 3d 628, 100 Cal. Rptr 152, 493 P.2d 880 (1972).

3. Art. 1, Sec. 27, Constitution of the State of California, added Nov. 7, 1972. 'All statutes of this state in effect on February 17, 1972, requiring, authorizing, imposing or relating to the death penalty are in full force and effect, subject to legislative amendment or repeal by statute, initiative, or referendum. The death penalty provided for under those statutes shall not be deemed to be or to constitute, the infliction of cruel or unusual punishments within the meaning of Article 1, Section 6, nor shall such punishment for such offenses be deemed to contravene any other provision of this constitution'. Adoption of this Amend-ment, of course, applied only to death penalty sentences imposed afterwards, due to the constitutional prohibition against ex post facto laws.

4. 356 U.S. 86, 78 S.Ct. 590, 2 L. Ed.2d 630 (1958). This case dealt with revocation of citizenship as a penalty, and it contains language written by the late Chief Justice Warren which is repeatedly cited by the California and United States Supreme Courts in dealing with the death penalty issue.

5. 493 P.2d at 894.

6. Three cases were decided simultaneously: *Furman v. Georgia, Jackson v. Georgia, Branch v. Texas* 408 U.S. 238, 33 L. Ed.2d 346, 92 S. Ct. 2726 (1972).

7. 408 U.S. at 263–64, citing *Weems v. United States* 217 U.S. 349, at 373 (1910), another precedent of great importance in the death penalty cases.

8. 408 U.S. at 270, citing *Trop v. Dulles* 356 U.S. at 100.

9. 408 U.S. at 303.

10. 408 U.S. at 341–42.

11. 408 U.S. at 361–62.

12. 408 U.S. at 363.

13. 408 U.S. at 371.

14. 408 U.S. at 309–10.

15. *Gregg v. Georgia* 96 S. Ct. 2909 (1976); *Jurek v. Texas* 96 S. Ct. 2950 (1976); *Profitt v. Florida* 96 S. Ct. 2960 (1976); *Woodson v. North Carolina* 96 S. Ct. 2978 (1976); *Roberts v. Louisiana* 96 S. Ct. 3001 (1976).

16. It is not impossible that, with change of personnel on the Court, the dissenting positions of Justices Brennan and Marshall may come to prevail, that the holdings in the *Gregg, Profitt*, and *Jurek* cases may thus be reversed. Such changes in personnel cannot normally take place until Justices die or retire. Thus, the issue of the death penalty returns to the forum of legislative reform for the foreseeable future.

PART II

Historical Aspects

Francesco Compagnoni

Capital Punishment and Torture in the Tradition of the Roman Catholic Church

IN treating of this subject, one can follow different avenues of approach, according to the purpose one has in mind. One can trace the historical development in its actual material reality and adduce evidence for and against the two penalties, seeking to demonstrate the motivations and historical needs on which they were based and coming into the present with a demonstration that 'today' the Church is absolutely opposed to torture and experiences many uncertainties when it comes to the death penalty. Or else one can decide to leave the dead to themselves and to trace the positions that have been adopted for and against the two penalties, in order to make use of the relevant arguments in the contemporary western context. This brief and incomplete outline will follow the second approach, relying on pragmatic reason and on the toleration of methods which is recognized today. The two retrospective points of departure will be, for torture, the 'Declaration against torture and all cruel, inhuman or degrading treatment' adopted unanimously (and therefore also by the Holy See) by the General Assembly of the United Nations (Resolution 3452[xxx], 9 December 1975), and, for the death penalty, Canon 984 of the Code of Canon Law, which declares unfit to receive priestly ordination 'any judge who has condemned someone to death' (n.6) and 'those who have assumed the office of executioner, as well as all those who, voluntarily and

directly, have assisted him in the carrying out of the death penalty'
(n.7). As support for these 'strange' canons, which were formulated in
an age when the Church was openly well-disposed towards capital
punishment, the 'Points for reflection on capital punishment' of the
Social Commission of the French Bishops' Conference, published officially in *Documents-Episcopat* (January 1978), will be of use.

By torture I understand exclusively here that which is inflicted by
public agents, whether it is covered by the legal code of the State or
carried out in fact within the framework of judicial or police powers. In
the history of the West it has been and is carried out either in order to
gain evidence or, following on a confession, to elicit the names of
accomplices or other information, or else, finally, as a method of
punishment (since the latter falls into the category of corporal punishment rather than into that of judicial torture, I will leave it out of
account). By capital punishment is understood this penalty as included
in the ordinary penal code of a State, excluding therefore military penal
codes in wartime, for example, or during states of siege. Consequently
my argument will refer to torture and capital punishment in so far as
they constitute part of the ordinary penal institutions' of a State. Finally, one observation of an historical nature must be made. In the
early Church, torture and the death penalty formed part of a whole
complex of moral problems which involved war, gladiators, criminal
judges, executioners and the military profession itself. It is to this
complex that the maxim *Ecclesia abhorret a sanguine* refers—the
Church abhors the shedding of blood. For reasons of space we can only
look at this problem strictly in connection with the two subjects already
mentioned.

TORTURE: THE HISTORICAL DEVELOPMENT [1]

It is unknown in the Old Testament and the New Testament mentions
it only incidentally when Paul (Acts 22: 24ff) points to the fact of his
own Roman citizenship in order to avoid being tortured (*lex Porcia*).
The first clearly stated position in the world of the Latin fathers is to be
found in the Montanist works of Tertullian (active between 197 and
207). In his *De Corona* (ch. 11) he asks how, among numerous other
forms of wickedness, could a Christian soldier avoid administering
torture, and in the *De Idololatria* (ch. 17) he asks, with pungent irony,
how a servant of God belonging to the judicial profession could avoid
causing torture to occur. In Lactantius too (active from about 305 to
323) are to be found some searing pages against torture; for example, in
Divinae Institutiones (V,20; VI,10), where he defines it as contrary to
human rights and every good, but he is referring to the tortures undergone by the Christians, for which reason his testimony does not seem

to me to have the same value for my purposes here as the preceding has. Augustine (*De Civitate Dei* 19,6, a work written between 412 and 416) does not in principle condemn the Roman institution of torture and with it the judge, but he makes a merciless indictment of the way it was applied, basing his argument on the certainty of the penalty applied to a man who is not yet known to be guilty, while a guilty person could undergo it without confessing. But quite apart from these three well-known and much quoted authors, it seems to me that other witnesses from the period, during which the Empire, having been made Christian in law, was to become Christian in fact, are also important. In the year 382, when Damasus was Pope, the canons of the Roman Synod to the bishops of Gallia (PL 13, 1181ff) state clearly in chapter 5, no.13, that state officials who 'have handed down death penalties, given unjust judgments and administered legal torture' cannot be regarded as free from sin. They have lapsed back into practices they had abandoned, as laid down in the traditional discipline. To gauge the import of this text, one should recall that there is a well-known imperial decree of the year 369 which confirms that it is forbidden to torture, except in cases of the crime of *lèse majesté,* those who because of their social class or newly-acquired dignity were already exempt from it. Now, twenty years after the synodal text, Pope Innocent I (401–417) wrote, in his *Epistola VI,* chapter 3, n.7: 'We have been asked how one should regard those who, after having received the sacrament of baptism, have assumed public office and administered torture or pronounced capital sentences. On this point nothing has been handed down to us'. But once God has conceded the use of the sword in penal law, the Church cannot criticize it. An in-depth analysis of this should be made, but I put forward the hypothesis that precisely round about the year 400, in spite of all the reservations of an Augustine, the penal practice of an Empire that had become Christian was progressively accepted. As is well known, there is an essential transition from the synodal text to those of Innocent and Augustine. The former is still at the level of Tertullian (can Christians administer judicial torture?), while the two later ones pose the question on the basis of the fact that now the State had an increasing number of Christian officials and that if all were to follow that ancient discipline, criminal justice would no longer follow its 'normal' course. The shift had taken place therefore in the problem and not only in the solution. With the barbarian invasions, however, torture declined, since for the new peoples in general trial by ordeal fulfilled the same function as Roman judicial torture. The available sources are therefore silent until the year 866 when the Bulgars were converted. Pope Nicholas I wrote to them (Denzinger 648) in response to questions concerning a number of dogmatic and moral matters, among them that of the torture that had been a usage among them before their conversion. It was the first time in western culture that the idea of suppressing torture was formulated! The confession ought to be spontaneous and torture is not permitted 'either by divine or by human law'. With such a procedure one obtains either nothing or else something uncertain. Giving evidence under oath or swearing on the Bible must take its place. Note that Nicholas does not recommend trial by ordeal either, which was defended in the same period by, for example, Hincmar of Reims.

The situation within the western penal code was, however, to change again very soon. The resurgence of the study of imperial Roman law in the twelfth century was to overthrow trial by ordeal and bring torture into force once more. It is true that one more splendid witness is still to be found in this century, but according to specialist historians such as P. Fiorelli, it represented by now a rearguard action. The text in question is the *Decretum Gratiani* (II, 15, 6 *quod vero*): 'Confession must not be obtained by torture, as Pope Alexander has written'. That it was the last stand for moderation and Christian consistency can be seen from section 15 of the same work, where in question V, chapter iv there is an almost certain reference to the torture of heretics. In the following century, the thirteenth, we will find the codification of what in practice had already occurred. The new centralized States reintroduced torture: Alfonso X in Castile, Frederick II in Sicily, Louis IX in France. England, blessed isle, remained the one exception. A parallel development occurred at the same time in the Church. In 1224 Innocent IV approved the penal legislation of Frederick II, and in 1252 (*Ad extirpandum*) he allowed that 'barring amputation and risk of death, heretics can be tortured in order to be forced to reveal their own wrongdoing and to accuse others, as is done in the case of thieves and marauders'. Judicial torture, therefore, complete, preventative and inquisitorial: it marked a return to the Roman penal system, which hinged on self-accusation and confession! The fact that this was a tragic and retrograde development can be verified in the moral part of the *Summa Theologica* of St Thomas Aquinas, the Secunda-Secundae which was written at the papal court in Viterbo at the end of the sixties of the thirteenth century. In question 64 (of injuries against persons) he speaks of mutilation, of the flagellation of children and slaves, and of incarceration, but not of torture. And yet it was known to him; indeed, in his *Expositio super Job* (X, 1–5) he says explicitly: 'It sometimes happens in fact that when an innocent person is falsely accused in the presence of a judge, the latter, in order to discover the truth, sometimes subjects him to torture, acting, when he does so, in accordance with the requirements of justice; but the cause of that is lack of human knowledge'. The text dates from the same time as the *Summa* and it reproduces Augustine's justification of torture as a tragic necessity for the sake of the common good. By this time little is wanting, and manuals for the *Inquisitio haereticae pravitatis* are about to make their appearance. Torture is officially accepted by the Church, even in trials for heresy, although its administration by ecclesiastics remains forbidden. It is the eternal struggle between inspiration and institution. We will have to wait until 1522 in order to hear the old teaching once again, notwithstanding the fact that in those very Carolingian years (Charles V, 1532) criminal ordinances of unheard-of cruelty were promulgated. The writer in question is the Christian humanist, Juan Vives, who in his commentary on *De Civitate Dei* (19,6) gives us one of the most Christian statements against torture: 'I am surprised that Christians hang on religiously, with the utmost attachment, to so many pagan practices, which are not only contrary to Christian charity and meekness, but also against humanity (as Lactantius and Nicholas argue). Augustine says that torture is in use for the sake of human society: but who could fail to note that he is speaking to and about pagans? But what in fact is this necessity—so intolerable and so deplorable that it should be purged if possible in floods of tears—if it is not useful and if it can be abolished without detriment to the public good? How is it that there are so many people (including the barbarians, as the Greeks are called), who allow a man whose criminality is in doubt to be submitted to the severest torture? We men, endowed with every humanitarian sense, torture men in order that they may not die innocent, although we are more sorry for them than if they were to die: often enough the torments are far worse than death . . . I cannot, and nor do I wish, to spend more time here on the subject of torture. . . . It has become a commonplace among rhetoricians to speak for and against it. But while what they have to say against it is very powerful, the arguments in favour are weak and useless'. The edition of Vives used here (TV, Froben, Basel 1551) has been carefully expurgated by an inquisitor, probably Italian, and this passage is one of the many that have been crossed out with strokes of the pen and rendered illegible by means of a piece of paper stuck on with care. This is a small point, but it is indicative of the extent to which even pious suggestions of clemency were rejected by the censorious authority of the Counter-Reformation. It will therefore be necessary to wait for a century before the discussion at the theoretical level is seriously developed and brought to a conclusion. The first work was that of John Graefe (Grevius), a Dutch Arminian pastor who published in Hamburg in 1624 his *Tribunal Reformatum*, a true *summa* of moral theology on the subject. To get an idea of the seriousness with which it is argued, it is enough to run through the index of the second book, devoted to arguments against torture: it cannot be justified from Scripture; it is against Christian charity and the natural law; evils which stem from it; its abuses; argument from the many who have committed suicide in order to escape it; and finally a long sequence of authoritative witnesses against it (including Vives and Montaigne). This work is followed by a number of others of Catholic provenance: F. von Spee, *Cautio Criminalis* (1631); J. Schaller, *Paradoxon de tortura in Christiana repubblica non exercenda* (1657); the Frenchman A. Nicholas, *Si la torture est un moyen sûr à vérifier les crimes secrets* (1682). But the masterpiece and at the same time the last of the efforts of these courageous and Christian men was the dissertation of C. Thomasius, *De tortura ex foris Christianorum proscribenda* (Halle, 1705). The thesis is that it is necessary to exclude torture from the criminal trials of Christians because it is against the divine and the natural law. This is demonstrated under three successive heads: it is against justice in general and is a disproportionate punishment; it is against the Christian sense of justice and proportion; specific arguments against the view of those who favour torture. The conclusion is that the prince can consider its abolition on purely political criteria, since theologically speaking and according to the natural law it is untenable—a position not of servile compromise but one which suits the state absolutism of the period. I said that the discussion was theoretically thus closed. In fact, the Illuminists, starting with C. Beccaria, *Dei delitti e delle pene* (Leghorn, 1764; French translation 1766), were to take up the first and third points of Thomasius' argumentation, without really adding anything else to it, but in so doing succeeding in getting prohibition introduced into legislation, Sweden and Prussia, under the young enlightened King, Frederick II, were the first to begin with partial abolition in 1734 and 1740 respectively (and therefore prior to Beccaria) and the process was to come to an end with the states which formally abolished torture during the post-Napoleonic restoration. In the meantime, the official Catholic Church was completely overtaken by events. On 3 February 1766 the Holy Office was to put Beccaria's book on the Index, and Alphonsus de Liguori, in the 1785 edition (the last non-posthumous one) of his *Teologia Morale* would have no difficulty in asking himself: 'What is permitted to the judge in the matter of torture?' Only one moralist, among the many I consulted, takes his stand, in a short note, alongside Thomasius, and that is the German Capuchin, R. Sasserath (*Cursus Theologiae Moralis*, 1787): 'All that I have said up to now on the matter of torture I took from the ancient practice and from the commonly-held opinion of moralists. Today, however, there is a passionate and many-sided discussion as to whether torture is an appropriate method to use. I for my part leave the question to be decided by the prince'. From the nineteenth century onwards no manual of moral theology would continue to refer to torture: it had been resolved in the seventeenth century as a theoretical problem and in the eighteenth as a problem of penology and judicial practice, without either the Magisterium or Catholic theologians having shown approval of this or even taken part in the discussion. Only in the twentieth century, after the First World War, would torture, a sign of barbarism, enter once more, not into legislation (the modern trial is exclusively presumptive) but into the practice of police interrogators, as well as of dozens of states. Against this practice, the Second Vatican Council (*Gaudium et Spes* (1965), 27,3) adopted a clear-cut position. Torture is against life itself, offensive to the dignity of the human person and a shameful practice. It is one of a group of actions which 'poison human society, though they do even more harm to those who practise them than they do to those who suffer from the injury, and which are, moreover, a supreme dishonour to the Creator'.[2] The argument is the same as that used in the United Nations Declaration against Torture: 'It is an outrage to human dignity and should be condemned as a denial of the ends of the Charter of the United Nations and as a violation of the fundamental liberties proclaimed in the Universal Declaration of Human Rights'.

TORTURE: REASONS FOR OPPOSING IT

Coming back to the propositions put forward at the beginning of this study, we must now ask ourselves what are the reasons adduced against torture by a whole body of thinkers and leaders in the Church. It seems possible to affirm that, until the end of the fourth century, Christian thought was against it all along the line, following in this the tradition which is opposed to all intentional shedding of blood. Arguments properly so called are lacking, and it is continually stated to be against human law and every divine commandment—*contra ius humanitatis, contra fas omne,* according to Lactantius, and Pope Nicholas I was to use the same formula (*nec divina lex nec humana admittit*), to which, for the first time in centuries, Pius XII would refer in his message to the International Congress on Penal Law in 1953. Augustine, on the other hand, offers us a genuine argument: it is a punishment prior to the judgment. That this is the genuine Augustinian argument can be seen from the above-mentioned commentary on the Book of Job of St Thomas Aquinas, in which the latter admits the punishment of an innocent person by means of torture. Finally, with Vives we have at the level of argument the development which fundamentally will also be found in Grevius and Thomasius: torture is contrary to charity and Christian meekness, as well as to every form of humanity, it produces endless evils, it is of no use for the purpose of discovering the truth, which is itself necessary for the protection of the community, and it can be eliminated without detriment to the latter. These arguments can be further developed on the basis of the knowledge we have of the effects/ultimate purposes of torture. The Amnesty

International report reproduces A. D. Biderman's list of means of coercion, in which the consequences of methods of coercing behaviour are grouped together under eight heads. From these one can deduce that torture tends to the disintegration and consequent annihilation of the psychic and moral personality, to the non-physical destruction, practically speaking, of the human person, with lasting results. This was confirmed experimentally by the Danish medical group of Amnesty International in *Evidence of Torture* (London, 1977). What we are concerned with, therefore, is a condemnation of a very serious penalty carried out by organs of the State which are not competent to hand down any penalty. On the other hand, the modern criminal trial, which turns no longer on the confession but on the evidence, does not derive anything useful to the purposes of honest investigation from a self-accusation elicited under pressure. But from a theological point of view it seems to me that greater weight can be attributed to another consideration: that the human person cannot, literally speaking, be sacrificed, in that by which it is most properly constituted, namely its rational freedom, to the need for a social system, the ultimate purpose of which is the welfare of all individuals. Without getting involved in considerations of personal utilitarianism, it seems to me that one of the central doctrines of theological anthropology is the absolute preeminence of man's dignity as a creature and as a Christian. Completely forgotten from the end of the twelfth century, this is the position taken up by such Latin fathers as Leo I and Gregory the Great, when they speak of the *dignitatis humanae naturae, substantiae, condicionis.* This dignity, autonomous in the face of any juridical institution or community whatever, is the reason why, even after the worst (and verified) crimes, there is always the possibility of repentance: the salvation promised by Christ is not limited by any need of the State. Were it to be so, this would be nothing more than the application of the axiom, 'the end justifies the means', the most powerful political expression of the cynical negation of all morality and of the Christian message.

THE DEATH PENALTY: HISTORICAL DEVELOPMENT [3]

The first testimony against it is again to be found in the *De Idololatria* of Tertullian (chapter 17): 'Even if he appeals to the power of the State, the servant of God should not pronounce capital sentences'. He maintains the same position in *De Spectaculis* (chapter 19), a pre-Montanist work. And Lactantius, in *Divinae Institutiones* VI,20: 'When God forbade murder, this referred not only to killing in the process of robbery, but also to the fact that one should not kill even in those cases in which it is considered just by men . . . Thus the just man, whose task it is to administer justice, is not permitted even to charge anyone with a capital crime, since it makes no difference whether one kills with words or with the sword: killing as such is forbidden'. In the same vein Minucius Felix (c. 225) affirms in the *Octavius* V: 'It is not right for us to assist in the killing of a man, or even to listen to an account of it; we are so opposed to the shedding of blood that we do not even eat the blood of animals that have been killed'. Even more explicit are the *Canons of Hippolytus* II, 16, which follow a very ancient Egyptian tradition. Speaking of the profession of the potential catechumen, they affirm: 'Let him who wields the power of the sword or the magistrate who wears the purple (criminal judge) renounce his office or else be excluded (from catechesis)'. At the beginning of the fourth century, canon 56 of the Council of Elvira (305) ordained that the duumvirate magistrates, even though they did not as a rule have to pronounce capital sentences, should not enter a Church during their year of office. Ambrose himself (340–397) reveals to us the Church's difficulty in this connection. He wrote, towards the year 385, to the magistrate Studius: 'Those who believe it is their duty to pronounce the death penalty are not to be found outside the Church; however, most of them do keep away from communion in the Eucharist, and for this they should be praised. I know that the majority of pagans consider it an honour to have brought back from their period of administration in the provinces an axe untouched by blood: what then should be expected of Christians?' Romans 13 recognizes the State's power to take life, but we should imitate Christ in his forgiveness of the adultress 'for it may be that the criminal will show hope of improvement; if he is not baptized he can receive pardon, and if he is baptized some form of penance' (Ep. 25). The former imperial official outlines clearly here the problem and the dilemma facing the Church, now integrated into the State. Augustine too was to follow this line of argument. After having recognized, in *De Libero Arbitrio*, that the death penalty is a commandment of God, he recognizes in Epistle LIV to Macedonius the need for severity, with the reservation, however, that Christian moderation should be able to have its say. 'Your severity is useful because it ensures our tranquillity; our intercession is useful because it tempers your severity' (Ep. 153). As in the case of torture at the beginning of the fifteenth century, the shift within the Church seems to be complete. In the text of the Roman Synod of 382, the old position was still adhered to, while Innocent I explicitly abandoned it. All the more admirable would be the teaching of Pope Nicholas I in the letter to the Bulgars mentioned above: 'You must act like the apostle Paul who, having been a persecutor, was converted and not only desisted from any application of the death penalty but gave himself up totally to the salvation of souls. Thus you must give up your former habits and not merely avoid every occasion

of taking life, but also, without hesitation and in every possible cir-
cumstance, save the life, both of body and of soul, of each individual.
You should save from death not only the innocent but also criminals,
because Christ has saved you from the death of the soul' (Ep. 97,
chapter xxv). Alongside this doctrine, which took up the earlier one
from the period after the barbarian invasions, the Church continued to
base its penitential discipline on the principle of conversion, and the
penitential books of the eighth and ninth centuries, speaking of capital
crimes, considered them only as sins. These, since there is always the
possibility of conversion, must be expiated according to their seriousness, but never avenged by means of the death penalty. In the twelfth
century, the *Decretals,* on the other hand, recognised explicitly that
the State (*gladius materialis*) has the right to administer the death
penalty, but that the Church (*gladius spiritualis*) has not, and that
clerics may not execute it. But the earlier attitude of mitigating influence on the part of the Church had disappeared, indeed for heresy and
magic the Church had to watch to see that it was applied. These texts
are the source of such remnants of opposition to capital punishment as
we find in the present Code of Canon Law, as was said at the beginning
of this article. As in the case of torture, everything was to happen in the
thirteenth century. Innocent III was to declare in 1208, against the
Waldensians: 'With regard to the civil power, we affirm that it is permissible to exercise the law of capital punishment, but with the proviso
that reprisals should not be taken out of hatred but in a spirit of wisdom, not inconsiderately but after mature reflection' (Denzinger 795).
This teaching would be received into the theology of the time. And
sixty years later Thomas Aquinas (*Summa Theologica,* II-II, 64, art.2)
was to systematize the solution: 'If a man is a danger to the community
and corrupts it through some sin or other, it is right and just that he
should be put to death in order to safeguard the common good. With
regard to Matthew 13 (the parable of the sower) there is no doubt that
one should pay attention to it, but as long as one is not running the risk
of putting to death an innocent man, one should bring sinners to justice.
As God himself does, so should human justice put to death those who
are a danger to others and reserve punishment for those who do not
seriously endanger others. Whenever he sins, man lapses from the
rational order and from his human dignity, which consists in the fact
that he is by nature free and exists for himself. When he abandons this
dignity of his, therefore, he lowers himself to the level of the animals
and so will be made use of to the benefit of others'. During the same
period, Thomas would again write (*Contra Gentiles* III, 146): 'The
common good is better than the particular good of a single individual.
One should therefore withdraw a particular good in order to preserve
the common good, which consists in the harmonious working of human

society. Some say that man can always improve as long as he is alive, and that he should therefore not be put to death but given the chance to repent: *haec autem frivola sunt*, these arguments, however, do not hold'. From this text we can, for our purpose, deduce that certain of Thomas Aquinas' contemporaries were against the death penalty for theological reasons, but that his own reasoning was based on the fact that the death penalty was regarded as the only means for protecting society when it is seriously threatened. This theory of St Thomas was to survive for centuries and it is basically still very widespread today, not only in Catholic circles. Even Duns Scotus (1308) allowed for capital punishment, but only in cases explicitly mentioned in Scripture, since God himself derogates there from the fifth commandment. Thus it would be permissible to put a man to death for murder or for adultery (*Summa Theologica*, Appendix 64 ad 2). Things were to remain at this point for centuries, even though there was always a certain latent opposition to it. For example, the Convention of the Gallican clergy in the year 1700 condemned as erroneous and heretical the proposition: 'Where is it expressly written that God has given kings and States leave to put delinquents to death? Is it to be found in Scripture or tradition, or is it an article of faith?' In the year 1786, the Abbé C. Malanima published in Leghorn a *Commento filologico critico sopra i delitti e le pene secondo il ius divino*, in which, aligning himself with C. Beccaria, he maintained that the New Testament revoked the Old Testament precept about putting the criminal to death. In 1867, the Abbé le Noir, in the second edition of Bergier's *Dictionnaire de Théologie* came out against the death penalty (a much-discussed question in his time, which saw the first abolitionist legislation), following Duns Scotus and the proposition censured by the Convention of 1700. F. X. Linsemann, in *Lehrbuch der Moraltheologie* (1878), para. 137, offers a superb assessment of the problem. His essential thought is that the right to inflict the death penalty cannot come from society and cannot simply be deduced from either the ends or the nature of punishment in general, but it is justifiable only in terms of extreme cases of legitimate defence. He admits the death penalty, however, only in cases of extreme social need—revolts, states of siege and so on. 'The legal suppression of the death penalty is only a political or cultural problem; from the point of view of the foundation of law, nothing is opposed to it'. J. Leclerq was to adopt the same position, though he approached it from a different direction, in *Leçons de droit naturel* IV (Louvain, 1955). 'The death penalty, like every other form of punishment, is only legitimate if it relates to the legitimate defence of the community. It does not find its justification in the right of the State to dispose of the life of its citizens, but only in social necessity. Human life is in itself inviolable as far as the State is concerned, just as it is in so far as individuals are concerned'. In their consequences, these two propositions correspond with that of C. Beccaria, who restricted capital punishment to cases of sedition and to those cases in which it was necessary to protect non-delinquents from the crime. More restricted positions are to be found in the last hundred years in 'minor' authors such as G. Coco Zanghy, whose *Il Cattolicesimo e la pena di morte* (Catania, 1874), was attacked in *Civiltà Cattolica* at the time, and the Austrian J. Ude—*Du sollst nicht töten* (Dornbirn, 1948)—both of whom argue from the fact that God did not give the civil authority any right to deviate from the fifth commandment.

CAPITAL PUNISHMENT: REASONS FOR OPPOSING IT

While it was not necessary to spend much time on the arguments against torture, since it is rejected by every legal State, it will not be possible to deal so briefly with the death penalty. It is still a feature of too many penal codes, and it is present above all as a possible and indeed desirable solution in the minds of too many Christians, in proportion to the increase in the incidence of crime, common as well as political. The tenuous succession of those who opposed the death penalty argued, for the first four centuries, on the same basis as in the case of torture: 'The death penalty is against the commandment of love received from Jesus through the apostles; its revengeful and retaliatory character is apparent in the act of execution. This point of view becomes comprehensible if one bears in mind the impression made by the atrocious executions of Christians. In fact, reference to the execution of Christians, who were condemned on account of their faith, comes up continually as a basis for argument. In respect of time, this position was limited to the first three centuries, to the period that is, in which Christianity was persecuted by the State. Once it was recognized, on the other hand, its relation to the laws of the state then in force changed'.[4] From the documents cited, we see, therefore, that the shift took place only towards the end of the fourth century and at the beginning of the fifth century, and then not without difficulty, precisely because it was contrary to moral experience as it was to doctrinal tradition. What was taking place, in fact, was the adoption of the position of the State, the clearest example of which would be found in St Thomas. Except that in the argumentation, as B. Schüller observed years ago, that which it is seeking to prove is taken as a given fact: the necessity of capital punishment. Elsewhere, St Thomas himself says clearly that: 'Human justice will put to death those who are a danger to others and will reserve other punishment for those who in doing wrong are not such a serious danger to others'. He admits, therefore, that only extreme danger to society justifies capital punishment. Our problem now is this: are there also theological arguments in favour? The document of the French episcopate mentioned at the beginning gives an, in my view, decisive response on the expiatory aspect of the matter, which is the only one to have theological relevance, since other possible foundations for it, such as vengeance, protection and deterrence have none: vengeance is contrary to any theological foundation, while the other two lie within the competence of the political authorities and do not need to be supported by any theological argument. 'The collective conscience feels that an assassination is a very serious, absolute disorder. It then appears to it that reparation should be made for this disorder by an equally absolute and definite act. And so one speaks of expiation—or in fact the phrase "he has expiated" is used after an execution. But strictly speaking can one say "he has expiated"? In reality this term is taken from religious language. Does it perhaps preserve in the collective conscience something of the pagan conception of those religions that permit human sacrifice? But the Judaeo-Christian tradition has given it its true significance, the only one that is acceptable today, given the conception we have of man. Expiation is understood within the perspective of sin, without its being automatically followed by the annihilation of the sinner. On the contrary, it is the latter who freely makes expiation: he recognizes that he has separated himself from God, confesses his fault and turns back to God, confident of receiving his mercy. His reconciliation with God and with the community is achieved through a life lived from that moment onwards in justice and in truth. To speak of expiation through the death penalty imposed by a tribunal is to distort the authentic meaning of the term'. One can say, therefore, that, taking Scripture as our point of departure, we put across a message which in this connection is based on three points: respect for the human person, the mercy of God, and Jesus as Saviour of mankind. From the theological point of view, therefore, in order to accept that in a relatively normal situation (not war, external or civil) the legal State has the right to use the death penalty, it is absolutely necessary to prove that it is impossible to find another way of preserving peace and justice. Starting from the fact that capital punishment is the most inexorable of all penalties, let us consider what are the purposes which the contemporary State recognizes punishment as having. Only if it can be demonstrated that such a punishment corresponds to those purposes, will it also be possible to 'delegate' to the State the power to pass so extreme a sentence on members of the sovereign people. Now punishment can have the following five purposes: (a) *satisfaction* (compensation) *to the victim*, the primitive purpose, which is to be found in the ancient practice of the private vendetta, and in the *lex talionis*; (b) *social deterrence*; (c) *intimidation of the delinquent himself*; (d) *protection of society and prevention of the criminal from doing further harm;* (e) *rehabilitation of the condemned man,* today regarded as the most important. With regard to the first general purpose of punishment, the death penalty is thought of in the majority of cases in terms of a life for a life. But this is clearly a misuse of language. One cannot cancel out the original, illegal, homicide with a second, legal, homicide: the family of the victim is simply given the feeling that vengeance has been carried out by the State, which is not in a position to give back to it the member it has lost. As far as the second motive is concerned, that is deterrence of potential perpetrators of serious crime, it remains to be proven that capital punishment is really effective. Above all, it is not easy to prevent capital crimes in this way, since the criminal who works out the arguments for and against in cold blood is only to be found within the covers of the thriller. And also because the irony observed by Voltaire still pertains—he relates that in England, during the many public executions which were carried out even for a multitude of minor offences, vast numbers of pickpockets would apply themselves to their profession. The third and fifth purposes evidently cannot be achieved by means of the maximum penalty, in so far as that ends up with the elimination of the subject himself. There remains the fourth motive, the protection of society and prevention of the same person from committing a similar crime again. But many means other than execution are available to the contemporary state. Imprisonment, for example (and this weakens arguments such as those of St Thomas Aquinas, in the sense that from the same first premise of the safety of society one can reach the opposite conclusion) understood as a satisfactory system, dates only from the second half of the last century. The first examples are to be found in Holland towards the middle of the seventeenth century. It is a typical case of moral reasoning: between the normative premise and the conclusion, also normative, there exists a second, descriptive premise, which, were one to change it, would obviously give one a different normative conclusion. But one can also proceed from the other end and consider the negative consequences which are the result of acceptance of the death penalty. In order to stick with what is concrete, let us see what arguments an organization which is calling for abolition of the death penalty adduces in support of its position. Take the Stockholm Declaration published by Amnesty International on 10/11 December 1977: the death penalty is frequently used as an instrument for the repression of racial, ethnic and religious groups, members of the political opposition or representatives of minorities (argument from legal abuse); execution is an act of violence and violence tends to provoke further violence (argument from the limitation of violence and hatred); the decision to use the death penalty and the execution of it does violence to each and every one of the individuals involved in the proceedings (the same argument from the dignity of the human person is to be found in the Code of Canon Law and *Gaudium et Spes*); it has never been proved that the death penalty has a particularly deterrent effect (argument from proven usefulness and unavoidable necessity); the death penalty increasingly takes the form of inexplicable disappearances, extra-judicial executions and political assassinations (argument from illegal abuse); execution is irrevocable and can be inflicted on the innocent (argument from difficulties in application).[5]

It seems to me, therefore, that the conclusions of the United States Justice and Peace Commission, in its study on the Church and the death penalty, should be accepted in their entirety: 'All these points (theoretical and pastoral) converge to form a pastoral attitude as follows: on account of the moral values at stake, and because of the lack of decisive contrary arguments, the abolition of the death penalty should be envisaged. In 1972, the Catholic Conference of the State of Indiana spoke of the growing awareness of the sacred character of human life. The American bishops expressed themselves on and acted vigorously in favour of life, against abortion and euthanasia. An internal logic will, therefore, have to lead Catholics, convinced that life is something sacred, to be consistent in its defence, and to extend this to include capital punishment. Such an attitude has meant that Catholics have found themselves standing side by side with Quakers, who have a long tradition of campaigning in favour of life'.[6]

Translated by Sarah Fawcett

Notes

1. P. Fiorelli, *La tortura giudiziaria nel diritto comune* (Rome, 1953), two volumes; A. Mellor, *La torture. Son histoire, son abolition, sa réapparition au XXe siècle* (Paris, 1949); F. Helbing-Bauer, *Die Tortur. Geschichte der Folter im Kriminalverfahren* (Berlin, 1926); R. Quanter, *Die Folter in der deutschen Rechtspflege* (Dresden, 1900); Amnesty International, *Report on Torture* (London, 1973); A. Mellor, *Je dénonce la torture* (Paris, 1972).
2. Cf. Department of Moral Theology of the Catholic University of Chile, a study of moral theology on torture, *Documentation Catholique* n. 1713, 6 February 1977, pp. 135–39.
3. H. Hetzel, *Die Todesstrafe in ihrer kulturgeschichtlichen Entwicklung* (Berlin, 1870); F. Skoda, *Doctrina catholica de poena mortis a C. Beccaria usque as mostros dies* (Rome, 1959); P. Savey-Casard, 'L'Eglise catholique et la peine de mort', *Revue de Science Criminelle et de Droit Pénal Comparé?*, nouvelle serie, 16 (1961), pp. 773–85.
4. G. Schmid, *Christentum und Todesstrafe* (Weimar, 1938), p. 36.
5. P. Bockelmann, 'Die rationalem Gründe gegen die Todesstrafe', in *Die Frage der Todesstrafe* (Munich, 1962).
6. *Origins*. NC Documentary Service, 9 December 1976.

Martin Honecker

Capital Punishment in German Protestant Theology

1. ARTICLE 102 of West Germany's Basic Law declares categorically, 'Capital punishment is abolished'. For present-day German Protestant theology capital punishment is therefore an issue of historical rather than immediate interest, except on occasions when violent crimes or terrorist attacks provoke calls for its restoration. Nevertheless the discussion of capital punishment in the German Protestant theology of the nineteenth and twentieth centuries may be instructive, since it opposed firm supporters and equally firm opponents, whose arguments are classical. In the nineteenth century Kant and Hegel, both Protestant philosophers, and the majority of Protestant theologians who followed them, strongly supported the death penalty, while Schleiermacher equally strongly opposed it. In the twentieth century the main opponent of the death penalty has been Karl Barth, followed by Ernst Wolf, while other Lutheran theologians (Paul Althaus, Walter Künneth, Gerhard Gloege) continued to argue for it years after its removal from the constitution. The restriction to the arguments for and against capital punishment presented in the nineteenth and twentieth centuries is reasonable because the battle against it, which has now gone on for some 200 years, did not begin until 1764, with Cesare Beccaria's book *Dei delitte e delle pene*. Previously it had been the general Christian view that the legitimate civil authority has the right to impose the death penalty on lawbreakers. Paul declared in Romans 13:4 that the ruler is God's servant for the good of mankind, and goes

on to warn: 'But if you do wrong, be afraid, for he does not bear the sword in vain; he is the servant of God to execute his wrath on the wrongdoer'. Article 16 of the Augsburg Confession of 1530, *De rebus civilibus,* 'On the Civil Order', consequently teaches that the 'due institutions and laws of good order' include the right 'to administer the law and give judgment by imperial and other customary law, to punish evil-doers with the sword and to wage just wars'. In other words, the reformers justified the imposition and implementation of capital punishment by the office of authority: as God's institution, civil authority has been given power to punish, the power of the sword.[1] Luther can even make the drastic claim that it is God himself who executes, avenges and beheads when legitimate authority does so. The reformers defended the legitimacy of the death penalty for enthusiasts and Anabaptists because they regarded the rejection of the death penalty by the enthusiasts as a fundamental challenge to and denial of the power and legitimacy of secular authority. Capital punishment was also justified on practical grounds as a punishment and deterrent. For such a view, based on the need to preserve order, the death penalty was a legitimate penal sanction, though Luther constantly recommended that the application and the severity of punitive action should be mitigated by rational love, *epikeia*.

2. The change in attitude to capital punishment during the enlightenment came about because the duty of the authorities to punish was no longer accepted as the only argument; the person of the offender was brought into the discussion. Capital punishment began to be held to be incompatible with the respect due to the humanity, first of the person punished, and later of those carrying out the punishment. In addition it was argued that the protection of society against violent criminals could no longer be guaranteed by capital punishment alone.

(a) This enlightenment claim that respect for humanity made it impossible to regain the death penalty was opposed by Kant and Hegel, who produced a new case for the death penalty which had a considerable effect on later periods. Kant's argument is different from that of Goethe, for whom abolishing the death penalty meant opening the state to chaos: 'If society forgoes the right to use the death penalty, the return of anarchy is at hand; the blood-feud is knocking at the door' (*Maximen und Reflexionen*, p. 685). The basis of Kant's argument is rather the 'moral personality' of the offender. He calls Beccaria's opposition to the death penalty 'conniving sensitivity from an affected humanity'.[2] In Kant's view capital punishment is required for justice' sake: the very freedom of the individual depends on his receiving the justice his action merits. Kant appeals to the idea of retribution, the principle of talion, when he says, 'Just as there is no identity in kind between a life, however burdensome, and death, so there is no equivalence between the crime and the retribution except death judicially inflicted on the criminal, but freed from any ill treatment which could make humanity, in the person of the sufferer, into a monster'. He continues immediately, 'Even if civil society, with the agreement of all its members, were to dissolve itself (e.g. a people inhabiting an island resolved to separate and scatter all over the world), the last murderer left in prison would first have to be executed so that everyone learnt what his actions were worth and blood-guilt should not cling to the people for not insisting on the punishment'.[3] Kant presses for the continuance of the death penalty with Old Testament remorselessness, claiming that it alone guarantees respect for the moral personality of the offender and the preservation of the moral order of the world. Hegel supports Kant, stating that it is the offender's 'honour' to receive his deserts in the punishment.

Kant and Hegel are the sources of the metaphysical penal theory which was to be so remarkably influential and effective in Protestant theology as a support for the case for capital punishment, the theory that punishment must expiate the violation of the moral order. For this the severity of the punishment must match the gravity of the crime. The purpose of punishment is to restore the law which has been violated, and it must be based on the order of justice, which is supra-individual. It is showing respect for the offender as a moral personality to make him participate, even against his subjective will, in the general objective moral order. The purpose of carrying out a death sentence is not just to preserve the authority and order of the State, but also to maintain the absoluteness of the moral order.

This metaphysical argument for capital punishment was adopted by Protestant jurists and theologians.[4] Notable advocates of the death penalty were the law professor Friedrich Julius Stahl (1803–61), with his book *Die Philosophie des Rechts* (2 vols, 3rd ed., Heidelberg, 1854) and the theologian Richard Rothe (1799–1867) in his much used *Theologische Ethik* (5 vols, 2nd ed., 1867–71). Other arguments besides the absolute status of the moral order which the State had to maintain were the idea of expiation and that of 'self-punishment', according to which the offender has inwardly to accept the punishment. On this theory, capital punishment is not just an act of expiation for the violation of the metaphysical order; it also has the function of arousing a subjective desire for expiation, an idea popularly known as 'gallows repentance'.

(b) This argument for the death penalty provided by German idealism won broad agreement in Protestant theology. Only isolated voices were raised against capital punishment among Protestant theologians. One of these, however, was that of Friedrich Daniel Ernst Schleiermacher (1768–1834) in his *Christliche Sitte*.[5] Schleiermacher claims that the demand that the offender acquiesce in his punishment is equivalent to asking him to agree to suicide. Schleiermacher also differs from German idealism in regarding the purpose of punishment not as the restoration of the moral order but as the restoration of the obedience of the person who has transgressed the law. This places punishment in the larger context of the moral education of the individual. It becomes an educational measure; in modern language, its purpose is resocialization, which means that the legal character of the legal penalty becomes less important for Schleiermacher. The purpose of punishment is to bring the person being punished back to obedience to the legal order, and not simply so that he passively accepts its effect on him, but so that he actively takes part in it. The purpose of punishment is therefore not only to protect the community; it should also enable the offender to take part in the community. The aim of this view of punishment is the integration of the offender into society, and the first step on this road is, for Schleiermacher, the abolition of the death penalty. As a comparison between Kant and Hegel on the one hand and Schleiermacher on the other shows, the discussion of the death penalty thus becomes a criterion of a general view of punishment and its aims. If the only purpose of punishment is to defend law and order and to preserve the moral order, capital punishment becomes the highest possible form of punishment. If, however, the purpose of punishment is held to be the reintegration of the criminal into society, capital punishment becomes meaningless. A dead man cannot reform. He is finally expelled from the community. This has the further consequence that society itself can no longer benefit from the reformation of the criminal. Central to Schleiermacher's support for reformative punishment is his assumption that punishment involves an interaction between the individual and society. Punishment must take account of the future life of the offender and of society. Karl Barth and Emil Brunner have adopted this idea when they advance society's complicity in crime as an argument against capital punishment. Behind the different views of capital punishment, therefore, lie different premises. As well as concern for the authority of the State, advocates of capital punishment are motivated by the absolute moral claim of the legal order, in some cases even by a religious view of expiation, and occasionally the deterrent effect. In this argument society, State and law have absolute priority over the individual, the offender. On the other side, opponents of capital punishment emphasize the priority of the individual over the legal order, and they also doubt both the deterrent effect of capital punishment and the assumption that capital punishment alone can ultimately guarantee the authority of the State.

3. (a) Whereas in the nineteenth century the opponents of capital punishment formed a small minority among Protestant theologians, in the twentieth century Karl Barth's fundamental theological rejection of the legitimacy of capital punishment as a legal sanction has won broad agreement. This is combined with greater allowance for the individual personality of the offender, with a total rejection of metaphysical theories of punishment, and also with the replacement of the idea of deterrence by the aim of resocialization and the orientation of punishment towards the human future of the criminal. The background to this development is a tendency away from a definition of the State in terms of authority and order, and in extreme cases the complete abandonment of the idea of the State for a view of society as a continuing process of socialization. The result is that Protestant social ethics no longer sees itself primarily as the representative of the civil power, but as the advocate of the individual, and so stresses the responsibility of the whole of society for those who undergo punishment.

Karl Barth (1886–1968) is the most important, but by no means the only representative of this view.[6] The other main figure is Ernst Wolf (1902–71).[7] Society's duty of solidarity even with the criminal as a fellow human being and its share in responsibility for the origin and growth of crime both exclude the right to use the death penalty. By passing the death sentence the State itself adopts a policy of lawless self-defence. The deterrent effect of the death penalty is doubtful. The death penalty is also incompatible with the aim of reforming the offender. But Karl Barth's main argument against the justification of capital punishment by the idea of expiation is the expiatory death of Christ, which was also used before him by the nineteenth-century Catholic theologian Franz Linsemann. 'Now that Jesus Christ has been nailed to the cross for the sins of the world, how can we still use the thought of expiation?'[8] Barth's argument is totally Christological: satisfaction for the sin of the world has been made once and for all in the crucifixion of Jesus Christ, and God has thereby taken the use of death as a punishment out of human hands. The argument from the expiatory death of Christ leads Barth to a complete abandonment of any use of the idea of expiation in penal law. Expiation was the work of God alone in the death of Christ. Since Christ, therefore, the only form of human punishment is educative and resocialising measures. If one excepts the Christological basis, which is, of course, to him fundamental, Barth's view of punishment here comes into contact with modern theories of punishment, though even within such modern critical theories there is disagreement about whether criminal law can become nothing but educative measures. There is also disagreement among theologians about whether it is possible to argue from the complete satisfaction made in Christ's death to the abolition of all human expiation. Nevertheless we must agree with Barth that the Christian faith in the crucified saviour leads to a critical attitude to all absolute theories of punishment and, while it may not totally eliminate human punishment, certainly makes it relative. Christian faith cannot accept either an absolute judgment or an absolute punishment as the standard of secular criminal law. A Christian view of punishment will also not generally be concerned with the past, but will feel an obligation to the future; it regards itself as 'reformation and reintegration of the guilty person into society'.[9] This, however, makes it impossible to give religious legitimation or theological sanction to capital punishment. Karl Barth thus allows the use of capital punishment, if at all, only in exceptional cases. Considerations of crime prevention may make capital punishment justified in the limiting case of high treason in war, just as in extreme circumstances Barth regards tyrannicide as a moral possibility.[10] On both occasions he regards it as an act of loyalty *in extremis*. Even the death penalty can be an extraordinary means of self-defence on the part of the community, though it has no place in a normal constitutional situation.

(b) The theological attack on the legitimacy of capital punishment provoked opposition from the Lutherans. The main figures here were Paul Althaus (1888–1966) and Walter Künneth (b. 1901). Against Barth these writers cite the doctrine of the two kingdoms, according to which the divine expiation made on the cross is not applicable to secular, earthly penal law. In support of capital punishment three arguments are advanced: (first) the sanctity of the moral legal order, (second) the idea of expiation and (third) the authority of the State. Künneth, for example, argues from the divine order of the world, which leads him to reject all humane theories of the purpose of punishment. His argument thus runs in the opposite direction to Barth's: according to him, the murderer breaches not only a human ordering of life, but also God's own ordering of the world. Künneth and Althaus see capital punishment as a restoration of this divine order: capital punishment is the restitution of an objective legal order, not an act of subjective expiation. It is thus independent of the offender's recognition of guilt or repentance. The third argument is based on the magistracy's authority to punish. 'The right to the death penalty confronts us with the ultimate metaphysical dignity and authority of the legal order of the State, and with the question whether the State regards itself as the custodian of the divine law of life or not'.[11] Künneth goes on to argue, 'On the basis of these fundamental theological insights, it must be asked whether it is right to celebrate the abandonment of the death penalty as a humanitarian advance, or whether it is not rather a moral weakness, an admission of sacrilege in the domain of government'.[12] Althaus comes to the same conclusion: 'For the Bible and the creed it is not a question of political judgment whether the State should continue to wield the sword of judgment or lay it aside, but a question of obedience or disobedience to the task God has given rulers'.[13] It is clear that all three arguments are unconvincing. The first tacitly equates the current system of government with the divine order of the world. However, once the historical mutability of any political system is recognized, it becomes questionable whether it is possible or justifiable simply to equate the system which happens to exist at a particular time with the claim of the moral order; we need only think of dictatorships or terrorist regimes which use the death penalty. The second argument can only make use of the idea of expiation in penal law by means of the principle of retribution, and the idea of retribution and respect for life are in contradiction. A secularized criminal law can also no longer rely on absolute theories of punishment. It can no longer base its arguments on what the offender deserves, but only on what we, as human beings, have the right to do to him. If a person has killed, it does not follow that we have the right to kill him. The third argument is connected with this. To carry out its task of securing and creating the peace of the earthly political community a constitutional State does not need the death penalty; it has enough other means at its disposal. Its authority does not depend on the passing and carrying out of death sentences. It would be an unhappy situation if the State could only be God's representative on earth by using the death penalty.

It should be pointed out that not all Lutherans accept this argument and its conclusions. Helmut Thielicke emphasises historical change in comparison with the acceptance of capital punishment by the Bible and the reformers.[14] Werner Elert argues for the abandonment of capital punishment because of excesses in the treatment of criminals in modern times.[15] Gerhard Gloege comes to a similar conclusion, though he suggests, not an absolute abandonment of capital punishment, but its suspension in view of the particular historical experiences of Germany.[16] In the background is the unsolved problem—whether one follows Karl Barth or not—of the meaning of retribution, guilt and expiation in secular penal law. It is by no means the case that all Barthians are against the death penalty and all Lutherans for it. The state of the argument is much more complicated, and attitudes to the death penalty are only partial indicators of membership of a theological school.

4. The theological evaluation of capital punishment faces a series of difficult questions, some unsolved.

(a) The fact that theologians often support capital punishment, which occasionally provokes horrified protests,[17] has one very obvious cause. Capital punishment is a familiar feature in the Bible and the theological tradition. The New Testament, however, merely takes it for granted as normal, but the Old Testament expressly demands it. The main proof text is Genesis 9:6: 'Whoever sheds the blood of man, by man shall his blood be shed; for God made man in his own image.' The passage does not, of course, contain an imperative; it simply describes a situation. And the legal principle of Exodus 21:12 'Whoever strikes a man so that he dies shall be put to death', relates to a cultural situation which has now become obsolete: it is simply impossible for nomads to keep a murderer in prison. Hermeneutical consideration shows that mere biblical literalism is not enough to justify the death penalty. Karl Barth says correctly, 'From the point of view of the Gospel there is nothing to be said for this institution, and everything against it'.[18] Barth distinguishes between Bible and Gospel. A decision based on a literal understanding of the Bible is impossible.

(b) Capital punishment has its roots in an archaic, magical or ritualistic outlook. The murderer has forfeited his own life. The order of life requires expiation. Execution is a sacral procedure. All these views are prominent in the Old Testament.[19] In the past, these assumptions of sacral law provided support for capital punishment. In Islamic countries it rests to this day on such a sacral system. In contrast, the Christian faith desacralizes the world, so that secular law becomes profane.

(c) The profaneness of State and society and the process of secularization since the enlightenment mean that criminal law can now be shaped only by secular aims. The claim that by the killing of the body or physical punishment the offender is able to make expiation, and that, if he repents, this saves his soul from the punishments of hell, is today a cynical argument. Equally unappealing is the proposal to sacrifice a human life to preserve the moral law.

(d) There is not a single rational argument for the necessity of capital punishment. This is the strongest argument against it. Mere considerations of utility cannot justify it, and the demand of a majority of the population for the death penalty certainly has no force as a moral argument. The deterrent effect is doubtful. Security can be achieved by other means. The reformation of the offender cannot be achieved by capital punishment. There is also the possibility of a mistake, which cannot be corrected when an execution has taken place. Rational criminology thus provides no support.

(e) And yet there remains a final, irreducible residue. Even if the criminal law must be influenced primarily by the shared future of criminals and society, essentially educational arguments alone are not enough to justify legal punishment. If these were the only arguments, lawbreakers who had been resocialized and no longer needed to be deterred, for example, politically motivated offenders or war criminals, could not be punished because they cannot be 'reformed.' We are thus forced to allow some place to the idea of 'just' retribution or 'just' expiation. In this context, capital punishment is the test case for the theory of criminal law in general. Criminal law shares in the problem that a community based on law may be placed in a situation in which it has to defend itself, in which the punishment of the lawbreaker becomes an unpleasant and unavoidable necessity.[20] Even Karl Barth talks, with reference to the execution of a traitor in war, of 'stern mercy'.[21] And Luther explains the duty of a Christian magistrate in these terms: 'But where there is true gentleness, the heart is wounded by any injury that afflicts its enemies. These are the true children and heirs of God, and brothers of Christ, who gave us this example on the holy cross. And so we see that a religious judge passes judgment on the guilty with pain, and his heart grieves for the death which the law imposes on them'.[22] Punishment can thus be a necessary 'alien work', an *opus alienum* of love and mercy. That is in no way an argument for capital punishment; the arguments against capital punishment are convincing. What it does is to make visible in capital punishment the problems inherent in any punishment insofar as it means inflicting injury.

(f) Anyone who is opposed to capital punishment must support the constitutional State as an alternative. The constitutional State as a protection against chaos is the condition which makes capital punishment unnecessary. The constitutional State is also the necessary condition for respect for the dignity of the human person. Capital punishment is not the only threat to human dignity and human life; another danger, increasingly serious today, is the use of torture. German Protestant theology, which in recent years discussed the case for and against capital punishment, has so far had little cause to give its attention to torture. In the future, however, the important question will be not just the abolition of capital punishment and the prevention of executions, but also the prevention of torture and opposition to its theoretical justification.[22]

Translated by Francis McDonagh

Notes

1. Martin Luther, *Werke,* Weimarer Ausgabe (WA), vol. 11, pp. 254–55 ('Von weltlicher Obrigkeit', 1523); vol. 19, p. 584 ('Vier tröstliche Psalmen an die Königin von Ungarn', 1526).

2. Immanuel Kant, *Die Metaphysik der Sitten* (1797), *Werke in sechs Bänden,* ed. W. Weischedel, vol. 4 (Darmstadt, 1956), p. 457.

3. Ibid., p. 455.

4. On this cf. Trutz Rendtorff, 'Die Begründung des weltlichen Strafrechts in der theologischen Ethik seit Schleiermacher'; Hans Dombois, *Die weltliche Strafe in der evangelischen Theologie* (Witten, 1959), pp. 9–97; idem, article 'Todesstrafe III', *Religion in Geschichte und Gegenwart,* 3rd ed. (Tübingen, 1962), vol. VI, cols. 926–929; idem, art. 'Strafe,' *Evangelisches Staatslexikon,* 1st ed. (Stuttgart, 1966), cols. 2240–43.

5. Friedrich D. E. Schleiermacher, *Die christliche Sitte nach den Grundsätzen der evangelischen Kirche im Zusammenhange dargestellt,* ed. L. Jonas (Berlin, 1843), *Werke* 1, 12, pp. 241–63, 248–49; Rendtorff, 'Die Begründung,' pp. 11ff.

6. Karl Barth, *Church Dogmatics,* vol. III, part 4 (Edinburgh, 1961), pp. 437ff.

7. Ernst Wolf, 'Todesstrafe': *Unterwegs 11, Naturrecht oder Christusrecht, Todesstrafe* (Berlin, 1960), pp. 37–74.

8. Barth.

9. Paul Ricoeur, quoted Ernst Wolf, p. 73.

10. Cf. Barth, pp. 448–50; Wolf, pp. 65ff.

11. Walter Künneth, 'Die theologischen Argumente für und wider die Todesstrafe', *Die Frage der Todesstrafe, Zwölf Antworten* (Munich, 1962), pp. 153–65, p. 164.

12. Künneth, p. 165.

13. Paul Althaus, 'Um die Todesstrafe': *Schrift und Bekenntnis,* Festschrift für S. Schöffel (Hamburg and Berlin, 1950), pp. 8–15, quotation from p. 10; cf. idem, *Die Todesstrafe als Problem der christlichen Ethik* (Munich, 1955).

14. Helmut Thielicke, *Theologische Ethik,* III (Tübingen, 1964), §§ 1463–1518, pp. 419ff.

15. Werner Elert, *Das christliche Ethos* (Tübingen, 1949, 2nd ed. 1961), p. 157.

16. Gerhard Gloege, 'Die Todesstrafe als theologisches Problem', *Verkündigung und Verantwortung, Theologische Traktate* II (Göttingen, 1967), pp. 184–256.

17. Wolf, p. 37; cf. pp. 39–40.

18. Barth, p. 446 (translation slightly altered).

19. Cf. Gloege, pp. 208ff.

20. Barth, p. 448.

21. Martin Luther, *Werke,* vol. 6, p. 267 ('Von den guten Werken', 1520).

22. Cf. the 'Statement on Torture' by the Central Committee of the World Council of Churches, 28 July–6 August 1977.

Clemens Thoma

The Death Penalty and Torture
in the Jewish Tradition

PRELIMINARIES

'TORTURE did not exist among the Jews'. This was Samuel Krauss's
conclusion after his studies of the Judaism of the Talmudic and
medieval periods.[1] Any attempt to establish how far this statement can
be corroborated, and how far it is a piece of apologetics, faces considerable difficulties. A normal one is the variability of the term 'torture',
which was given different interpretations at different times. In terms of
Jewish history torture may be described as cruel torment going beyond
the measure of punishment recognized by the religious law and in
conflict with the spirit of the revealed and implied law, inflicted on one
or more persons to produce death, to force a confession or agreement,
or to compel them to perform a certain action. Harsher customs prevailed in the past than today, and the penal practice of Old Testament
Judaism was far more humane than that of the non-Jewish Near East
or the Graeco-Roman world, but we shall not discuss this point in de-
tail.

A special difficulty in assessing traditional Jewish penal practice is
the fact that the term 'Judaism' is an umbrella term. Various, often
widely diverging, groups have, regarded, and still regard, themselves
as Judaism. If we wish to obtain a general view of Jewish penal principles, forms of execution and terms of imprisonment and torture in
order to discuss them in Christian theology, it is a mistake to take our
information predominantly or exclusively (as is sometimes done) from

the time of Jesus. This is a temptation because this period contains the crucial event for Christianity of the passion of Christ, which took place against the dark backcloth of a bloody Roman justice and similarly harsh practices of torture and execution in zealotic, Sadducean and Hellenistic Judaism. On the other hand, the Jewish communities of the middle ages and subsequent periods have taken their norms mainly from the discussions, interpretations and decisions of the groups of rabbinic scholars active between A.D. 70 and 550–600 in Palestine and Babylon. The main concern of rabbinic Judaism, which is what these groups constituted, was the updating and modification of biblical and early Judaic penal practice. The results of this rabbinic work can be found scattered through the Babylonian and Jerusalem Talmuds, in various collections of midrashim and in other individual rabbinic works, either studies of the religious law or stories.[2] From the early middle ages until today there have also existed in Judaism, alongside the rabbinic tradition, two other strands, a philosophical one which kept its distance from the rabbinic tradition, and a mystical and esoteric one which has tended to be at odds with it. In recent times Judaism has also undergone radical transformations as a result of the appearance of new movements and of the founding of the state of Israel in 1948. Nevertheless, the decisions of the rabbinic scholars on the religious law remain for Judaism an important basis on which religious decisions are taken and from which reforms begin.

Unfortunately the current scholarly investigation of the rabbinic penal and legal norms is mostly not very accessible.[3] Halakhic studies are today conducted mainly within orthodox Judaism, and published in Hebrew, and have adopted an approach based on internal Jewish systematics rather than a critical or historical one.[4]

RABBINIC PENAL DECREES AGAINST CRUEL AND FALSE JUDGMENTS
AND TORTURE

The Hebrew Bible, and especially the Pentateuch, contains many calls for capital punishment and non-capital penalties, and for the rabbinic scholars these were both an obligation and a burden. On the one hand, they wanted their legislation and their discussions to embody absolute obedience to the God of the biblical revelation; they regarded law as deriving from God.[5] On the other hand, however, they also had anthropocentric concerns and ideals. They were aware both of the inhuman justice practised in areas outside Jewish rule and of the violation of human nature and human dignity in the earlier Sadducean judicial practice, which had kept strictly to the letter of the Bible.[6]

1. Precautions against death sentences and executions

The following sentences from the mishna are characteristic of rabbinic attitudes to the imposition of the death penalty: 'A council which carries out an execution once in seven years is known as a murderous one. Rabbi Eleazar ben Asariah (c. A.D. 100) said it is to be called murderous if it carries out an execution once in seventy years. Rabbi Tarfon and Rabbi Akiba (both c. A.D. 120) said, "If we had sat in the council, no man would ever have been executed" ' (mMak 1, 10). In the view of L. I. Rabinowitz, this passage makes clear that 'the whole tendency of the rabbis was toward the complete abolition of the death penalty'.[7] It is true that many rabbinic disquisitions on people who are to be executed, flogged, etc., in such and such a way for such and such reasons are primarily attempts to avoid, as far as possible, the implementation of the capital punishments (and the other punishments) prescribed by the Bible, and to make inhumane attendant circumstances impossible. To allow these efforts to be judged, we shall now contrast some biblical penal laws with the most important rabbinic penal laws.

The two most common forms of execution in the Old Testament are stoning (e.g., Lev. 20:2; 24:13,16; Jos. 7:25) and burning (e.g., Lev. 20:14; 21:9). There is also the punishment known as 'cutting off', where the form of death is not always clear (e.g., Ex. 12:15,19; 30:33,38; 31:34; Lev. 17:4,9). Murder, blasphemy, magic, false worship, obstinacy, unchastity, etc., are usually punished by death in the Old Testament. In such cases the participation of the whole people in the execution is typical. In Joshua 7:25–26, for example, it is reported that 'all Israel' stoned Achan and burned his possessions for his theft of the booty which had been placed under the ban ('devoted'). The Old Testament also has non-capital punishments. The most important is flogging, forty lashes (Dt. 25:1–3), though cutting off a hand (Dt. 25:11–12) and beating (Neh. 13:23–29; Sir. 33:25–27) also occur. There are frequent warnings against omitting or reducing this and other punishments: 'your eye shall have no pity' (cf. Dt. 7:16; 13:9; 19:13,21). Punishment in excess of the legal prescription is also punished. Anyone who beats a slave to death is also to be punished by death (cf. Num. 35:21; Ex. 21:20). Anyone who injures another in a fight so as to leave permanent physical damage is to have the same injury inflicted on him as a punishment (Ex. 21:23–27).

The rabbinic writings know four main forms of death penalty, stoning, burning, strangling and beheading. In addition there are the non-capital penalties of flogging, beating and imprisonment. To ensure as far as possible that no one should ever have to be sentenced to death by a Jewish religious court, the rabbis laid down legal conditions intended to make sentence and execution of the sentence impossibly difficult. A death sentence can only be passed by a small Sanhedrin (twenty-three members) and, in particularly serious cases, by a large Sanhedrin (seventy-one members, mSan 1, 4–5). Witnesses at the trial of a capital charge are subjected to a thorough examination to test their reliability and fitness. Certain grounds allow one party in the trial to reject the other party's witnesses. Relatives of the accused, representatives of professions of ill repute, women, children, and so on, cannot be called as witnesses (mSan 3,1–4; 4,5; bSan 8b; SifDev 190). Public notice must be given of a proposed execution, to leave possibility for an appeal against the penalty even after sentence (mSan 6,1; bSan 43a). It is almost impossible to determine how far these and other legal precautions against harsh and unjust religious justice were simply theoretical academic proposals and how far they influenced the behaviour of the Jews of late antiquity and the middle ages. In one respect at least they remained purely theoretical, since in the whole period from A.D. 70 to 600 the rabbis had no political possibility of exercising the jurisdiction on capital crimes conferred on them by the Bible.

2. *Precautions against the extortion of confessions*

In bSan 9b; bYev 25b there is a halakhah which was intended by the rabbis to make impossible any use of torture to extract a confession in connection with a judicial proceeding. This halakhah was composed by Raba (c. A.D. 320) on the basis of the injunction of the Torah, 'Make no wicked man a witness' (Ex. 23:1 in the rabbinic reading). It runs: 'A man is close to himself' (another possible translation is 'A man is related to himself') and 'no man can declare himself wicked'. The main emphasis is on the second part, 'No man can declare himself wicked'. This law also exists in a more general formulation: 'No man can give evidence about himself' (before a court) (bKet 27b). An accused's confession is therefore not decisive either in his conviction or in his acquittal. Only fit and reliable witnesses are decisive (cf. also above, 2,1). If he faced conviction the accused would be a witness in his own case, and therefore unable to be objective. He would be—in the halakhic terminology—his own relative. But close relatives are excluded as witnesses (mSan 3,1.4). He would also be, at least by presumption,
a wicked man, and wicked men are also ineligible as witnesses (mSan 3,2–3). Under the Jewish religious law it would therefore be useless and pointless to extract a confession from an accused by torture.

3. Concern for bodily integrity

In bSan 52b there is a reminiscence of an execution by burning shortly before the destruction of the Temple in A.D. 70. Rabbi Eleazar ben Zadok tells how, as a child, he saw in Jerusalem a priest's daughter who had been found guilty of harlotry, was surrounded with bundles of brushwood and burnt. In other words, he had witnessed a Sadducean form of education which strictly followed the letter of the Bible (Lev. 21:9; cf. also Jub. 30:7–10). On hearing his story, his fellow scholars expressed their displeasure at this cruel performance of the biblical commandment. The rabbinic way of burning an offender is described as follows in mSan 7:2: 'The procedure to be used against the person to be burned is as follows. He is placed in dung up to his knees. A hard cloth is placed in a soft cloth and wound around his neck. One executioner pulls it (one end of the cloth) towards himself and the other pulls it (the other end) towards himself until the condemned man opens his mouth. A metal wire is heated and poured (the liquid hot metal) into his mouth so that it goes into his bowels and burns his bowels'.

The wrapping of the rope which forcibly opens the condemned man's mouth in a soft cloth is a rather trivial indication of the (rather crude) concern for the greatest possible humaneness at an execution. More striking is the whole method of burning as described here. It does not agree with the biblical method, and can only be understood against the background of the rabbinic scholars' concern to preserve the offender's body as far as possible undamaged. The burning is only carried out in the outwardly invisible bowels. This concern also appears in the rabbinic methods of stoning and strangling (mSan 6:4–5; 11).

The rabbis' reasons for concern with the bodily integrity of those executed derive from their theology, which they took from the Pharisees, the most characteristic feature of which is the doctrine of bodily resurrection after death and the presence of the image of God in man. Like the Pharisees (cf. Acts 23:6–9), the rabbis preached belief in the resurrection of the dead, arguing that this belief was required by the Torah. They regarded the resurrection not as the mere immortality of the soul, but as the resuscitation of the whole man (*tehiyyah, anabiosis*), who forms a single psycho-physical entity.[8] The human body, in this view, is the determining feature of human nature, and therefore resurrection will take place with the body. The body of a criminal must as far as possible be kept undamaged for the resurrection. To emphasize this, in the context of sentencing to death or a physical punishment the rabbis translated the biblical word *nefesh,* the inward part of a person, the spirit or 'soul', as 'body' (bYom 74b, following Lev. 23:30). The second theological doctrine to which the rabbis attached particular importance was the presence in man of God's image (cf. Gen. 1:26–27), which was visible and tangible in the human body. The Bible ordered that the corpse of a person who had been stoned had to be hung on a tree. The biblical reason why the body should hang on the tree only for a short time (not beyond sunset) is as follows: 'For a hanged man is a curse of God' (Dt. 21:23). The rabbinic tradition generally understood this verse as meaning 'a hanged man is a curse for God', and connected it with the doctrine of the image of God which was visible in the human body. A disfigured, battered, mutilated body was an insult to God; it was as if it showed God as mutilated and so dishonoured him. The rabbis feared that the deformed body hanging on the tree could lead to disparaging thoughts about God's exaltedness and perfection (cf. mSan 6:6–7; bSan 46b; TPsJ on Dt. 21:23; Rashi on Dt. 21:23). A third reason for the rabbis' concern for the bodily integrity of the offender was the commandment to love one's neighbour. A passage of the Talmud says, 'The scripture says, "Thou shalt love thy neighbor as thyself" ' (Lev. 19:18). 'Choose a beautiful death for him' (bSan 52b). The term 'beautiful death' (*mitah yafah*) means not only an execution involving the least possible pain but also one involving the fewest possible disfiguring injuries.

RESTRICTIONS ON THE POSSIBILITIES OF TORTURE

1. Fear of Torture by Non-Jews

'Non-Jewish courts execute without carefully investigating (guilt)' (bYev 25b). This description was an annihilating criticism of contemporary non-Jewish penal practice: Jewish courts, in contrast, were said to carry out a careful investigation into the guilt of the accused, and to pass just sentences. The rabbis had a profound distrust of contemporary non-Jewish courts, and they had every reason to. tAZ II,4. Zuckermandel (p. 462) says, 'Neither steel nor implements of steel are to be sold to them (non-Jews), nor is steel to be sharpened for them. Nor are shackling blocks (instruments of torture for crushing the legs), ropes, transport vessels (?) or iron chains to be sold to them'. This prohibition of trade with non-Jews was based, as the context shows, on the fear that the non-Jewish authorities might use these implements as instruments of torture against Jews.

2. Non-Jews and Slaves as Objects of Torture

The rabbinic Jews interpreted certain biblical descriptions of God's courts as indications that disobedient non-Jews were subject to the law of torture. The following passage from a midrash is typical: 'A parable. A matron went into a palace and saw rods and clubs hanging there, and was frightened. The occupants of the palace said to her, "Do not be afraid. Those are for the slaves. You are here to eat, drink and be honoured" '. So is it with the community of Israel. When they heard the passage about the tents and the plagues (cf. Ex. 7–11) they began to be afraid. Then Moses said to them, 'These things are for the nations of the world. Your lot is to eat and drink and practise the Torah' (BamR 13,4). The midrash also gives the reason why, in the parable, all the instruments of torture are meant for the Gentiles. According to Genesis 8:21 ('the imagination of man's heart is evil from his youth'), it argues, God has no high opinion of the qualities of non-Israelites. In this connection the midrash says, 'Woe to the dough (meaning non-Israelite mankind, who act against the law of God) which the baker (God) judges to be bad. That is why we read, "Set up courts for scoffers" ' (Pr. 19:29). This midrash does not claim that Jews are allowed to use instruments of torture on non-Jews. Its origin has to do much more with observations about torture in the states of late antiquity. The author of the midrash concluded from this that torture was typical of wicked non-Jewish circles. Non-Jews were doomed to torture. The term 'slave', used in the midrash for non-Jewish peoples, also refers, however, to abuses practised at the time by individual Jews which were the sort of thing non-Jewish slaves could permit themselves. Although the Mosaic law protects slaves against abuse (cf. Ex. 21:2; Dt. 15:12–15; 24:14–15), in Sirach 33:25–29 beating and whipping, hard work and fetters are recommended to force slaves to do their work. Since the book of Sirach was highly regarded by the rabbis (cf. bBQ 92b) it is not surprising that rabbinic writings should also include occasional disparaging remarks about slaves and calls for harsh punishments (cf. bShab 32a; PRE 29).

3. Pressure to Act Rightly

Judaism is primarily a religion of 'orthopraxy': the law is to be done. Jews must try to make their lives conform with revelation. Secondarily, however, orthodoxy is inherent in Judaism. In all periods it was regarded as extremely important that all Jews should hold the correct teachings about God, revelation and the people of revelation.[9] Since orthopraxy has a higher status than orthodoxy, it may be assumed that there was never a tendency in Judaism to force anyone to profess the orthodox Jewish faith. Doctrinal unity in Judaism was always relative. On the other hand it is reasonable to ask whether any form of torture existed in Judaism to compel action in conformity with revelation. There are in fact some cases in which coercive measures which might well be described as torture are sanctioned by the rabbinic religious law.

The first case has to this day remained purely theoretical. In Leviticus 1:3, according to the specifically rabbinic reading of this verse, it is said that the man who brings a bull as a burnt offering must 'make the offering to the Lord of his own will'. In bAr 21a–b (on mAr 5,6) and in bYev 106a (on mYev 2,9) it is argued that the clearly expressed will or agreement (*dacat*) of the worshipper is an essential requirement for the validity of the burnt offering. Otherwise the sacrifice is invalid and becomes a sacrilege. Since cattle represented great material value, the rabbis had to take into consideration abuses which could creep into the making of a burnt offering of a bull. A debtor could, for example plead an obligation to make a burnt offering to avoid having to pay or having the animal seized. Or a benefactor could pay for the debtor's sacrificial bull. In all these cases the full agreement of the person liable for the burnt offering could be obstructed or he could get out of agreeing. If the person did not clearly express his willingness to make the offering in such circumstances, the rabbis ruled that the following had to happen: 'Let him be forced until he says, "I agree" '. In the rabbinic writings the verb used here and in the following cases, *kph, kp', kpj, kpp,* means 'bend', 'make to stoop', 'force down', 'compel', 'force'. It is mental or moral pressure which could be reinforced by physical means such as beating, though the pressure was not supposed to go so far that the will was broken and consent once again became impossible. In bRhSh 28a there is a discussion of the case in which 'the Persians' 'forced someone', and the view is taken that no agreement was given.[10] The formula 'Let him be forced until he says "I agree" ' also occurs in connection with divorce and with 'the sodomitic kind'. The rabbis held that in certain circumstances the wife had the right to demand a divorce (*get*) (cf. mKet 7,10). However, this right can only be exercised with the husband's agreement. If he refuses to agree and so puts the wife in a situation which is impossible humanly and under the religious law, the court can force him to agree (bAr 21a–b; bYev 106b).[11] By 'sodomitic kind' the rabbis meant totally selfish behaviour. bBB 12b has a discussion of a case in which two people buy a field which borders on a piece of land which had been left to one of them. This partner can, on the rabbinic view of the law, insist that he should be regarded as the owner of that half of the field which borders on the land he has inherited. If the other suffers no disadvantage from doing this favour he can be forced to agree.

4. Measures against incorrigibles

A ruling of the mishna for Jews who have already committed a number of crimes so that in the biblical view heaven itself would long ago have been expected to intervene (to cause sudden death), runs as follows: 'Anyone who has been flogged before the court on numerous occasions is to be taken to the prison (lit. 'the vault') and given barley to eat until his stomach bursts' (mSan 9,5). In bSan 81a this ruling is interpreted as follows: 'It concerns flogging in connection with being cut off from the people, so that the man is in any case destined to die. Since he voluntarily submits, we let it (death) approach'. It is possible that imprisonment as a penalty was used on a few occasions among the Jews of Babylon and Palestine between the fourth and sixth centuries A.D. In modern terms, the feeding tortures connected with it, which could lead to death, are to be regarded beyond doubt as torture.[12] The rabbis, however, were not interested in the feeding tortures. What they were really doing was looking for ways of creating conditions in which heaven could decree the death of the incorrigible. They found the biblical justification for their procedure in Exodus 32:20, according to which Moses mixed the remains of the melted down golden calf and gave them to the Israelites to drink, and the worshippers of the calf suddenly died.

CONCLUDING REMARKS

From late antiquity until today, very many Jews, individually or as groups, have had to endure torture at the hands of anti-Jewish authorities which led to death or mental collapse. To describe this torture which came from outside they used the term *innuy/innuyyim*. This term is formed from the piel form of the biblical Hebrew word *anah* means torment, oppression or humiliation. In rabbinic writings *innuy* occasionally occurs in connection with asceticism, especially exaggerated asceticism, 'by which the body is brought low' (bYom 74b). The internal Jewish punishments and coercive measures discussed in this article, however, are never described as *innuyyim*. The implication is that there is no comparison between the internal Jewish measures and anti-Jewish tortures or judicial murders.

The vigorous and consistent opposition of rabbinic scholars to cruel and over-hasty executions and all forms of sadism associated with non-capital punishments continues today to win the highest admiration, which it fully deserves. The most important religious motives of this opposition were the belief that man is made in God's image and the belief in the resurrection of the whole man, and obedience to the revealed law of the Old Testament, and in particular to the commandment of love of neighbour. Full success in defending the rights of all accused or convicted persons against torture and unjust punishments was only granted to the rabbis in the case of capital punishment. In the case of merely disciplinary penalties associated with actions requiring consent and in that of the punishment of slaves and incorrigibles, they did not always attain the highest degree of humaneness. Descriptions of floggings, beatings and terms of imprisonment are ample evidence of this.[13] The temptation to base 'Law and Order' on religious law and to enforce it uncompromisingly remained present in Judaism. The successors of the rabbis—notably Moses Maimonides (1135–1204)—made vigorous attempts to counter this temptation. In revising the rabbinic penal code, all later Jewish religious authorities were anxious to make impossible any legal or illegal tortures which had come to light, and to reduce still further the severity of the penal code. Their attitude was one of fidelity to the rabbinic penal maxim: 'If anyone destroys a man it will be reckoned to him as if he had destroyed a whole world. And if anyone preserves a man's life, it will be reckoned to him as if he had preserved a whole world' (mSan 4,5).

Translated by Francis McDonagh

Notes

1. *Talmudische Archäologie*, vol. 2 (Leipzig, 1911), p. 497.

2. The abbreviations of rabbinic works (and of relevant journals) which appear in this article follow Siegfried Schwertner's volume of abbreviations of the *Theologische Realenzyklopädie* (TRE) (Berlin, 1976). (Where quotations from scripture are not from the RSV, they represent the author's German version. *Translator.*)

3. Particularly helpful to outsiders are the articles published in the *Encyclopaedia Judaica* (EJ) (Jerusalem, 1971) on the traditional penal practice of religious Judaism. Cf. esp. Saul Berman, 'Law and Morality', *EJ* 10, pp. 1480–84; Haim C. Cohen, 'Capital Punishment', *EJ* 5, pp. 142–45.

4. This applies, for example, to the modern standard work on halakhah, the *Encyclopaedia Talmudit*, which began to appear in 1947 and now consists of sixteen volumes. For our subject vol. 14 in particular is important (Jerusalem, 1973), esp. the following articles: Ḥetzqat kashrut, pp. 26–39; Ḥayyabe mitot byde shamayim, pp. 580–603; Ḥayyabe mitot bet din, pp. 603–26; Ḥayyabe malquyyot, pp. 626–714.

5. On obedience and humanity as features of the rabbis' ethical views, cf.

Feliz Böhl, 'Gebotserschwerung und Rechtsverzicht als ethisch-religiöse Normen in der rabbinischen Literatur (Freiburg im Breisgau, 1971); Joseph Dan, 'Ethical Literature', EJ 6, pp. 922–32; I. Herzog, Judaism, Law and Ethics (London, 1974).

6. Cf. A. Büchler, 'Die Todesstrafen in der Bibel und der jüdisch-nachbiblischen Zeit', MGWJ 50 (1906), pp. 539–62, 664–706; Zeew W. Falk, Introduction to Jewish Law of the Second Commonwealth, vol. I (Leiden, 1972); Martin Hengel, 'Mors Turpissima Crucis. Die Kreuzigung in der antiken Welt und die "Torheit" des Wortes vom Kreuz', Festschrift Käsemann (Tübingen, 1976), pp. 124–84.

7. 'Capital Punishment, Practice in the Talmud', EJ 5, pp. 145–47, quotation from pp. 146–47.

8. Cf. W. E. Nickelsburg, Resurrection, Immortality and Eternal Life in Intertestamental Judaism (Cambridge, 1972).

9. On the view of orthodoxy and 'orthopraxy' in Judaism, cf. J. Neuner, The Rabbinic Traditions about the Pharisees before 70 (Leiden, 1971); Clemens Thoma, Christliche Theologie des Judentums (Aschaffenburg, 1978).

10. On the meaning of kph cf. J. Levi, Wörterbuch über die Talmudim und Midraschim, 4 vols (Darmstadt, reprint 1963), esp. vol. 2, pp. 376–78, 382–83.

11. Cf. Ludwig Blau, Die jüdische Ehescheidung und der jüdische Scheide-brief (Budapest, 1911; reprint, Farnborough, 1970); Miachel Krupp (ed.), Aka-rin, die Mischna: Text, Übersetzung, Erklärung (Berlin, 1971), pp. 80–81. According to yNed IX, 42c, force may also be used in marriage when one party refuses the other conjugal rights.

12. Cf. S. Krauss (ed.), 'Sanhedrin', Giessener Mischna (1933), p. 259; Ḥayyabe mitot byde shamayim, see n. 4 above, p. 380.

13. Cf. bKet 86a–b; ySuk 5,2 (55b); bQid 81a; and Haim E. Cohen, 'Flogging', EJ 6, pp. 1348–51.

Mohammed Arkoun

The Death Penalty and Torture
in Islamic Thought

I AM bound to make it clear from the very beginning that I do not share
the current opinion, according to which the traditional religions are
ultimate authorities of knowledge and intangible systems for the regula-
tion of individual and collective existence. All that I shall attempt to do
in this article is to contribute to the renewal of thought about the death
penalty and torture, taking as my point of departure the Islamic example.

I shall begin by a brief outline of the sociological and historical
conditions that prevailed at the time of Mohammed and the origin of
the Quran. I shall then go on to indicate the important positions of
religious law or *Sharî'a* with regard to murder (*qatl*) as an offence and a
sanction. Finally, I shall provide a (too rapid) survey of the theoretical
problems raised by the *Sharî'a* today in the Islamic societies that are
confronted by modernization.

'URF AND SHARÎ'A

THESE two Arabic words refer to an anthropological distinction. *'Urf*
is the local common law in force in various ethnic and cultural groups
not only before, but also after the appearance of the phenomenon
known as Islam. *Sharî'a*, on the other hand, is the system of legal and
religious norms and categories based on Quranic texts, the authentic
prophetic traditions (*Hadîth*), the consensus of the community (*Ijma'*)
and reasoning based on an analogy with the explicit rules of the Quran

and the *Hadîth*.[1] The Muslim state, which may have had a khalif, a sultan (in the Ottoman period) or a simple emir at its head, has always attempted to introduce the *Sharî'a* in place of the local common laws, but the latter have resisted this change all the more effectively, as their regulations and customs have been transcended by the teaching of the Quran, especially those connected with punishments.

These verses from the Quran may perhaps serve as an illustration:

'Those who wage war against God and the one whom he has sent and who do everything to sow disorder on earth will be punished by being put to death, crucified, having opposite hands and feet cut off or being banished far from their own country. They will be held in ignominy in this world and the next and will be cruelly tortured' (V. 33).

'Produce evidence from four of you against those of your wives who have been guilty of depravity (= illicit sexual act). If they bear witness against them, enclose them inside your dwellings until they are visited by death or God grants them a way of salvation' (IV. 15).

'We have prescribed for them in the Torah: an eye for an eye, a nose for a nose, an ear for an ear, a tooth for a tooth, life for life. All injuries are subject to the law of talion. A charitable renunciation of the right to retaliate is equal to an expiation of one's sins. Those who do not judge in accordance with what God has revealed are unjust' (V. 45).

'O believers! The law of talion is prescribed for you in cases of murder: a free man for a free man, a slave for a slave, a woman for a woman. The one who is pardoned by his brother for having murdered will have to pay damages in good grace in conformity with the custom. This is a mitigation and a mercy on the part of your Lord. Anyone who transgresses after that will be cruelly punished' (II. 178).

Many more examples could be given of verses in the Quran that go back to practices in Arab society that was subject to what is known in the Quran as the *Jâhiliyya,* in other words, to ideas and forms of behaviour that are uncivilized, as opposed to the ideal, humane and emancipating norms taught by God and his prophet. The emphasis in this primitive teaching is on cases of permanent and bloodthirsty conflicts—rivalries between families, clans and tribes involving theft, robbery and murder; women responsible for the honour of the family or the clan (*'irdh*), in other words, the life of men and women who are responsible for the power of the clan to defend itself or attack its enemies (with the consequent insistence on endogamic marriage and inbreeding often restricted to parallel cousins); an endless cycle of revenge (*tha'r*) because every murder calls for another and so on.

The Quran represents in every case an attempt to mitigate the harsh collective attitudes imposed by a sociological apparatus without any form of political control. The overall direction of its teaching is towards a respect, even an exaltation of the human person (*al-insân*), who is created by God and responsible to him for grave sins (*kabâ'ir*), one of which is murder (*qatl*). One striking example of this mitigating effect is the prohibition of the barbarous Arab custom allowing the father of a family to bury his young daughters alive (*maw'ûda*; VI. 137, 140; LXXXI. 8) for obscure reasons. Another is the general prohibition of murder (IV. 29, 92–93): 'The believer has not the right to kill another believer except in error. Anyone who erroneously kills a believer is bound to set a believing slave free and to pay the family of the victim the price of the blood, unless this is charitably renounced. If the victim belongs to an enemy clan and is still a believer, the murderer will have to set a believing slave free. If the victim belongs to a clan with which you are allied by a pact, the murderer will have to pay the price of the blood to the family and set a believing slave free or otherwise fast for two consecutive months as an expression of repentance before God, the all-knowing, wise one. Anyone, however, who intentionally kills a believer will suffer the punishment of eternal hell'.

The Quran, then, protects human life, introduces distinctions and confirms the norms and attitudes that had been in force for a long time in the common law or *'urf*. It is valuable at this point to summarize the position of the Quran with regard to the elaboration of the *Sharî'a* during the first two centuries of the hegira.

1. The death penalty was explicitly prescribed in the case of 'those who wage war against God and the one whom he has sent', the wife who was guilty of an illicit sexual act, intentional homicide (the law of talion) and apostasy (*murtadd*).

2. More generally, grave sins (*kaba'ir*), regarded as direct transgressions of the will of God, would be punished on the Day of Judgment and there was no right of intercession or possibility of remission (II. 48). Torture, torments, eternal fire, cruel punishment, anger and God's curse were again and again invoked in connection with these sins.

3. All hardened unbelievers (*kuffâr*) and believers who had broken with God because of serious sin were to suffer the death penalty and be tortured. These rules regarding punishment are in fact an expression of a system of protections for the emerging Muslim community that was threatened by the existing tribal society with its clan solidarities. It is worth noting, however, that the new community made use of the same methods for the formation of alliances and oppositions in order to establish itself. To do this, contingent and secular norms and practices were raised in the Quran to a transcendental level (the price of blood, stoning, the emancipation of slaves and so on). The Islamic doctors and lawyers continued to take the historical and social circumstances surrounding the Quranic interventions (*asbâb al-nuzûl*) into account, but they at the same time neglected to study the theological difficulties raised by the legal verses.

THE TEACHING OF THE *SHARÎ'A*

Attempts to define what is now called the 'Islamic' position regarding justice, property, authority, religious freedom, the death penalty and so on frequently result in confusion, partly because a search is made at random in the Quran, the *Hadîth* and the *Sharî'a,* all three being regarded as undisputed and indisputable authorities. In this article, I shall confine myself to the *Sharî'a.*[2]

It should be borne in mind that the teaching of the *Sharî'a* has two different sources. Until the second half of the eighth century (= the second century of the hegira), the politico-religious leaders (khalifs, governors and judges) settled cases by considering the data of the local *'urf* and what they knew of the sacred texts. From about 780–800 onwards, however, a body of legal writing was developed. This moved in two directions. On the one hand, a series of theoretical writings about legal decisions (*ahkâm*) emerged and, on the other, a *corpus juris* which was used by the judges was elaborated. This means that the *Sharî'a,* which was raised to a transcendental level by the later theories of the fundamental sources (*Usûl al-fiqh*), is in fact a historical construction with close links with the political and cultural data and the customs and practices of the Arabo-Islamic world during the first two centuries of the hegira.[3] The principles contained in the Quran are incorporated into this construction, but, as I pointed out briefly above, the teachers of the law have given very little attention to the theological difficulties involved in this operation.

The basic difference between the Quran and the *Sharî'a* is that the first makes use of contingent data in order to emphasize the relationship between God and man and to fill men's minds with a consciousness that there is a world beyond this world of events, values, norms and possessions. All this is clothed in mythical language and structure which opens the way to problems rather than excluding them. The second, on the other hand, systematizes, within the framework of a code of law, the pragmatic solutions that were adopted at an early period. It is understandable, then, why it is wrong to call norms that have been included in this code and perpetuated by an inflexible teaching Islamic.

The penal code and the death penalty in particular are good examples of this. The various categories of men dealt with under different headings in the Quran (ethical, spiritual, eschatological and so on) are systematized in the *Sharî'a* from a strictly juridical point of view. The *Sharî'a* also divides humanity into Muslim believers and non-Muslim unbelievers[4] in the following way: Muslims are either freemen or slaves, non-Muslims include the people of the Book (= Jews and Christians) and unbelievers; among the people of the Book, there are those who agree to pay the tax (*jizya*) and those who refuse to pay and who therefore are likely to be involved in a legal action leading to the death penalty. In lawsuits, the form of the proceedings, the severity of the sentence passed and the type of punishment inflicted differ according to the offence and according to the category of person tried. (For example, he may be crucified, stoned, strangled or hanged.)

The blood of a Muslim believer can only be shed because he is guilty of the crime of apostasy, deliberate homicide or an illicit sexual act. Torture and cruel methods of putting to death are excluded. In practice and according to the socio-political context, the usual punishment is a hundred strokes of the whip for fornication, but there is a difference of opinion among authors about the application of this penalty with or without stoning, which should be continued until the person dies. A slave has to suffer only half of this penalty, because he lacks the quality of *muhṣan*, which is possessed only by the free Muslim. (The free Muslim is *muhṣan* if he is legally married, but has never committed an illicit sexual act and is protected by a penal law against a slanderous charge of fornication or *qadhf*.) In this context, it has also to be pointed out that a distinction is made in the *Sharî'a* between the rights of God and the rights of man. The rights of God (*huqûq Allah*) include apostasy and failure to observe prayer, fasting or the *zakât* (the prohibition of certain foods). These sanctions are imposed by God and cannot be changed, modified or remitted. The reduction of the penalty for a slave can be explained by the fact that God has no material interest in mind. The rights of man (*huqûq âdamiyya*) are treated differently and, if they are violated, a material compensation has to be made (talion, the price of blood and so on). Offences committed against honour are treated as mixed.

The inequality and variety of the penalties awarded to Muslims and non-Muslims can be explained not by political or racial considerations, but by the religious criterion on which the hierarchy of legal status is based according to the *Sharî'a*. The highest position in this hierarchy is that of the male Muslim who has reached the age of puberty, is mentally healthy, free and legally married. He is protected by the penal system as the one who is most responsible in the eyes of the law inaugurated by God (*mukallaf*). If he does not obey the laws of God, he can also be punished by the death penalty. Next in this hierarchy is the free Muslim woman who is *muhṣana*. If she commits apostasy, she is forced to return to Islam, but she does not suffer the death penalty. She is followed in the hierarchy by the male Muslim slave and then the female Muslim slave, unbelievers who are protected by the Muslim sovereign (*dhimma*; these are mainly Jews and Christians who are tried by their own law-courts except in cases where their offences concern Muslims), foreign unbelievers who are temporarily protected on Islamic territory and finally unbelievers who are at war with Muslims.

It is true that some of the distinctions and ideas that were current in early Arab societies are perpetuated, but the *Sharî'a* gives them an explicit legal status by defining them according to the categories of pure and impure, sacred and profane, divine and human and true and false in the order of revelation and therefore also in the order of knowledge and practical conduct that result from that revelation. The word *Sharî'a* means the clearly defined way followed by believers and *fiqh* means religious knowledge par excellence or an understanding of the deep meaning of religious teaching. These two terms themselves provide a good insight into the values and attitudes discussed here.

Some of the attitudes leading to the application of certain penalties can be understood in this context. For example, the law of talion does not apply to the Muslim who kills a *dhimmî* who is protected by the Muslim sovereign, whereas the *dhimmî* who is the accomplice of a Muslim in a murder is put to death, while the Muslim himself only has to pay the price of the blood (*diya*). The *diya* paid by the *dhimmî* is half that paid by a Muslim. The *dhimmî* who is guilty of blasphemy against God, the prophet or the angels incurs the death penalty.[5] The life and the possessions of the foreign unbeliever are not protected by any law, although he may be granted a temporary security (*amân*) by a Muslim, who is a responsible man or woman. In such a case, the foreigner is treated as a *dhimmî*.

Space prevents me from saying much about the attitudes towards the struggle that Muslims have to conduct to defend the rights of God, in other words, the so-called 'holy war' or *jihâd*. *Jihâd* is waged against extreme oppressors (*bughât*) who appeal within Islam to a different form of 'orthodoxy' (see the Quran XLIX. 9). *Jihâd* is also waged against all unbelievers who refuse to be converted or to pay the *jizya*.[6] In such a case, the blood of all men capable of bearing arms who have not yet been taken prisoner is declared lawful.

Should we include under the heading of torture the penalty against theft—the amputation of the right hand and the plunging of the stump into boiling oil to prevent bleeding? The first time that the offence is repeated, the left foot is cut off, the second time it is repeated, the left hand is cut off and the third time it is repeated, the right foot is cut off. Only the Hanefites insist on the amputation of the left foot for the second offence and then they apply another punishment, such as imprisonment.

Our modern sensitivity and our concern to respect the physical and moral integrity of the human person lead us to reject such punishments. It should be noted in this context, however, that Pakistan and Libya have followed the example set by Saudi Arabia in reintroducing these classical penalties. This brings us to our final section, in which we consider the present-day tensions between the *Sharî'a* and modern legislation.

THE *SHARÎ'A* AND MODERN LEGISLATION

Generally speaking, legislation is slow to reflect the development of customs, feelings and ideas. This is so throughout the world. In the particular case of Islam, it is possible to speak not only of conservatism, but also of a recurrence of the traditional form of law in the ideological context of a revival of the 'authentic' Arabo-Islamic spirit, as a reaction to the cultural invasion of imperialistic western ideas into the Arab world. In fact, the leaders have tended to make use everywhere of the only effective psycho-social weapon available to them to control the irresistible rise of popular movements basing their call for autonomy on the *'urf,* to some extent penetrated with the teaching of the *Sharî'a*. The present nationalist movement is in favour of a reactivation of the ideological operation brought about by the teachers of the law at the beginning of the Abbasid dynasty. The decisions taken with regard to the law by the judges and administrators between 670 and 730 or thereabouts were transformed into a body of teaching, the *Sharî'a* in its 'Islamized' or 'sacralized' form, at a later stage by the theory of the fundamental sources of the law. This Islamized *Sharî'a* is historically false, but it helped to bring about a socio-cultural integration of the Muslim city. This is why the states are nowadays anxious to preserve the theoretical fiction that has become a myth since the eighth century (second century of the hegira). Every time that a modification is suggested in legislation, the divine nature of the *Sharî'a* is stressed and its unchangeable aspect is solemnly reaffirmed.

Given these conditions, it is not difficult to understand why it was possible to insist on the death penalty in Egypt in 1977 for the apostasy of a Muslim. The present lawgivers are unable to set aside attitudes that are contrary to the present-day consensus of opinion on the basic rights of the human being. What is more, he can often contribute to a strengthening of traditional beliefs that inevitably slow down the process of renewal. We are bound to admit that public opinion lacks the means to influence the development of ideas and the laws that embody them. The death penalty and torture depend above all on the good will of the leaders if they are to be abolished. If those leaders have the necessary intellectual development, the right religious convictions and good political aims, they may either reactivate the penal enactments of the *Sharî'a* or encourage such punishments as imprisonment or fines, leaving the passing of sentences to the judges. (This is the *ta'zîr* of the classical law.)

It is quite common for rural or Bedouin people to continue to apply the ancient norms of the *'urf,* especially in cases of sexual offences where the honour of the family is involved.[7] The authorities are usually strict when there is a question of eliminating the early law of revenge leading to useless killings. More often, however, the death penalty does not have the same force in modern Muslim societies as it does in western countries. On the one hand, the violence does not take the same form, nor is it so virulent as in the industrialized societies of the West. On the other hand, the people of the Muslim societies are hard pressed by the ordinary everyday tasks of living and concerned with urgent political, economic and psychological struggles involved in the radical changes in their traditional family and social relationships. They are therefore less able to take part in humanitarian discussions than intellectuals living in the West.

Space prevents me from analyzing the conditions that may lead to the reapplication or the suppression of the death penalty and torture as an indicator of the movement of the Muslim people towards increased human dignity. To judge from recent experiences in various socio-political contexts, it would seem that what has been achieved in certain places is not irreversible, nor is it necessarily well adapted to the biological and socio-historical state of man today. In other words, it is not sufficient simply to abolish the death penalty as a sanction imposed by justice or torture as means of enslaving men's wills. There are also the collective executions, the taking of innocent hostages, the blind acts of terrorism that have been 'legalized' each time by the 'interests' of a nation, a state or a group. If violence has biological roots and links with the sacred and if 'human beings are historical structures' and the result of 'an evolution and an odd job',[8] then we must no longer approach the problem of the death penalty and torture as a purely ethical or religious phenomenon which disguises its real nature or as a traditionally legal question. It is basically a biological and socio-historical threshold that mankind is very painfully crossing.

Translated by David Smith

Notes

1. See J. Schacht, *An Introduction to Islamic Law* (Oxford, 1964).

2. As a body of law, it should be distinguished from the Quran, just as the Christian gospel has to be distinguished from canon law.

3. This historical and critical presentation has been rejected by Muslim fundamentalists as a weapon used by 'orientalists' against Islam. It is based mainly on the work of I. Goldziher, J. Schacht, C. Chéhata and others.

4. It is interesting to note that mankind was divided by the Second Vatican Council into non-Christians and non-believers.

5. See A. Fattal, *Le statut légal des non-musulmans en pays d'Islam* (Beirut, 1958).

6. For this tax, see 'djizya', in the *Encyclopédie de l'Islam*, 2nd edn.

7. See J. Chelhod, *Le droit dans la société bédouine: recherches ethnologiques sur le 'urf ou droit coutumier des bédouins* (Paris, 1971).

8. F. Jacob, 'Evolution et bricolage', *Le Monde*, 6, 7 and 8 September 1977.

PART III

Psychological and Social Aspects

Pierre Viansson-Ponté

The Call for the Death Penalty

WHENEVER a crowd gathers outside a court where a murderer is on trial, a prison where he is sent or at the scene of the crime, it is never to call for mercy, but always to call for the death penalty. If a man has killed another, he must pay for it by dying himself. That cry, an instinctive one, has echoed down the ages. In the recent past, there were signs that it was getting weaker, but now, suddenly, it is being heard again. In several countries, the death penalty has been abolished or at least a decision has been taken not to apply it any more. It is precisely in those countries that campaigns are being conducted, by the press, members of the government and even political parties, for its re-introduction. In other countries, the death penalty is still in force and sometimes—as in France—applied. In these few countries, campaigns in favour of its abolition are being conducted with increasing discretion, because they go counter to the majority. There are even associations pleading for the widespread use of the death penalty, their members making more noise now than their opponents.

Despite the good will, the generosity and even the passion of those who want to see it abolished and remain abolished, it would be foolish to pretend that there is no movement in favour of the death penalty in Europe and America at present, both for its continuation and for its re-introduction.

The reasons for this can be grouped under two headings. One group of reasons is clear and relatively easy to elucidate, the other consists of hidden and often hardly conscious reasons and is therefore less easy to clarify. I do not claim to be exhaustive in this article, but will try to examine the causes as fully as possible.

In any research into causes such as this, one is bound to make affirmations and take impressions as one's point of departure. Even if I have not listed references at the end of this article, my affirmations and impressions are well founded on facts and proofs. They are based, for example, on a reading of opinion polls, careful observation of public reactions and tendencies, a knowledge of what lawyers, sociologists and criminologists are currently saying about this question, a following of the press, books, articles and so on and a correspondence which has taken every event, every attitude and everything said connected with the death penalty into account.

As sociologists, moralists and journalists all know only too well, there is hardly any other question that gives rise to such intense passions and so many firm judgments on the part of men and women who would hesitate to express themselves so confidently about other topics.

CRIME AND CRIMINALITY

The public is quite convinced that crime is constantly increasing and that there are more murders committed now than ever before. This is wrong, completely wrong. Without entering into the polemics that are almost always aroused by statistics, it is possible to say that there are certainly fewer murders and blood-crimes in the developed countries and democracies or at least there are no more than there have been in the hundred or hundred and fifty years that have passed, even taking into account the growth in population.

What has certainly increased is crime of other types—theft, housebreaking, obtaining property by false pretences, aggression of various kinds, hold-ups in which the aggressors do no more than threaten, scuffles and various other forms of violence. 'You might as well be hanged for a sheep as for a lamb'—sayings of this kind have given rise to the popular conviction that the man convicted of a crime involving aggression today will be the gangster or even the murderer of tomorrow. There is a good deal of confusion today about crime of the first kind and criminality involving murder. There are many criminals who did not in the first place aim to kill, but who have been led to do so in the course of committing the crime.

Violence, torture and summary execution are again and again denounced—rightly, unfortunately—in countries with a right-wing or a left-wing totalitarian government by the 'free' countries of the world and these phenomena give the impression that we live in a dangerous world where human life counts for very little. Even accidents—on the road, in the factories and so on—contribute to this spirit of resignation in the face of general insecurity and a universal threat. Everything is involved in a confusion of blood and tears and all rational discussion is therefore excluded. The widespread conviction that crimes of blood will continue to increase in number and violence throughout the present period is too deeply rooted in the public mind for denials, however soundly based, to be seriously considered.

THE PART PLAYED BY THE MEDIA

Another recent area of change is the extraordinary emphasis given to every crime by the media and especially by the audio-visual media. It is particularly striking how many newspapers, for example, nowadays regard it as their special responsibility to give a full account of the 'facts' of a crime, to conduct an enquiry in parallel with that of the police and in this way to involve their readers in the pursuit of the criminal. These newspapers reach perhaps several hundred thousand people. Information on the television, on the other hand, reaches millions, even tens of millions. The crime that is in the limelight at any given time is repeated in the newspapers and on the screen again and again, described in all its details and subjected to a great deal of comment, so that the readers', viewers' and listeners' attention is captured and retained.

The ideal murder, it could be said, is one in which the victim is an average man, not well off and unimportant, or a child from an ordinary environment. This is because the reader or viewer likes to identify himself or herself with the victim—what has happened to him (or his kid) may also happen one day to me (or to my child). This kind of crime is, of course, happening every day—more anonymous passers-by, little tradesmen and employees are killed than bosses, bankers or government ministers. On the other hand, the death of an important or public figure—a star, a singer, a financier, a manager who is well known or an industrialist—calls other reflexes into play which are equally profound: if that can happen to him or her, who is important and protected, could it not happen to me as well, who am of no importance, but much more vulnerable?

In the same way, we are permanently influenced by detective novels and thrillers published in instalments, full of revelations and repercussions and containing a form of reality which goes far beyond fiction. As the media almost always fasten onto what is of secondary importance and neglect the essential aspects in any case, they provide us, under the pretence of informing us, with a 'distraction' in the Pascalian sense of the word which, they hope, will help us to forget our worries, a diversion which will exempt us—and even prevent us—from giving our serious attention to the real problems.

About two years ago, after a particularly horrifying crime—a child was kidnapped and killed in cold blood by the kidnapper before even any attempt had been made to negotiate a ransom—the most popular presenter of the most widely followed 'news' programme on French television (Roger Gicquel, TF 1, 20. 00) began his broadcast by saying in a melodramatic tone and with his face showing signs of grief: 'France is terrified tonight'. With those few words he had in fact broadcast the seeds of fear in the minds and hearts of many of his twenty-five million viewers.

PSYCHOSIS AND FEAR

Distress and fear—an old man is murdered, a child is kidnapped or an innocent person is attacked and millions of old people, parents, ordinary citizens and countless others tremble. A real psychosis of murder, aggression and violence spreads, nourished by the brutality of human relationships in the great urban centres, the traditional suspiciousness of country dwellers and all the stresses and strains of modern life in general. Rumour is simplified, exaggerated and twisted and this also has its effect on the collective subconscious mind.

The findings of the American scholars Allport and Postmann in their researches into rumour are well known. One of their experiments was to show a short film to several spectators, who watched a white man with an open razor in his hand talking in a calm and relaxed way to a large Negro. Afterwards, each of the spectators was asked to tell the story of the film to someone who had not seen it, the second person was asked to tell it to a third person and so on. It was on average by the fourth person that the razor had changed hands from the white man to the Negro and by the seventh that the Negro—or one of the Negroes, since in certain cases the story ended with as many as four—was attacking the white man.

The murderer—both the real and the imaginary murderer—is always a monster. And every crime presupposes a murderer. If the real murderer is not identified and arrested, a suspect is. A poisonous snake is crushed and a bloodthirsty wolf is beaten to death. The criminal or the suspected criminal must die.

It is better not to doubt, object or dispute the question. For example, it is better not to suggest that the only person who could commit a crime like that is someone who is unhappily mentally sick. Or that we do not know whether he did it alone—he must have had accomplices and these should be found before he alone is accused. Or that it is not absolutely certain whether or not he is guilty and that it may be one of those cases in which even a confession does not mean very much.

If you do this, you will let loose a flood of passions and be accused of preferring the murderer to his victim, of being the murderer's accomplice, at least in the moral sense. Those whom you have upset will even go so far, perhaps, as to wish that you could experience what the victim or his family has experienced or that a member of your family could experience it. If that happened, you would not go on sowing doubt and talking about understanding the suspect or the accused. The murderer is a threat to society and society must protect itself, that is all.

Hang, draw and quarter him! This angry and violent reaction is inspired by panic and at the same time by a kind of cheerful sadism which has a stupefying effect on many law-abiding citizens, calm and otherwise moderate heads of families and middle-aged men who always uphold law and order. 'He will be questioned in court. There will be all kinds of expert statements, pleas and pretences in an attempt to acquit him. Well, we only get what we deserve. Monsters like that man ought to be destroyed at once. Or rather, they ought to be made to suffer for a long time before they are put to death, so that they pay for it and as an example to others'. Some people go even further: 'I would not cut his head off with the guillotine. I would cut one hand off first—the one that killed—then the other and then each of the legs that he used to run away. Then, when he had suffered enough, I would finish him off.' This kind of bloodthirsty and terrifying statement is unfortunately heard only too often, with frightful variants. One sometimes even reads such statements, sometimes brutally frank and at others veiled in allusions, written by men who, one thought, were well balanced and considerate.

'Put him to death!' This is the cry of doctors whose profession is to fight to save life, lawyers whose task is not to condemn, but to defend, moralists who should lead public opinion and who bear a particularly heavy responsibility when they champion the cause of death and finally churchmen. Yes! In France there is at least one prominent churchman, a Dominican whose main work at present is to demand the death penalty for murderers on the basis of the argument that by sparing their lives we are preventing the expiation of their sin and the possibility of their redemption!

A FRINGE DISCUSSION

This, however, is not all by a long way. Many people think that the discussion about the death penalty is of secondary importance, an almost ludicrous fringe discussion. Why debate so seriously about principles when millions of human lives are threatened, lost in wars, famines, internal political conflicts and massacres of horrifying dimensions? Of what real importance is the legal death of a few incurable criminals who are a danger to society compared with these large-scale deaths? Not to speak of the many different kinds of dramas that strike down millions of innocent people . . .

In France, there have been sixty-four people executed for legal crimes (common law) since 1950. In twenty-eight years, then, hardly as many people have died because of the death penalty as are killed on the roads in a single summer weekend—and those are innocent people. So, instead of crying about the fate of these murderers, let us try to save lives, bring our minds to bear on things that matter. Let us not waste any more time or energy on discussions that will result in nothing. What difference does it make—two or three executions each year?

It might be valuable at this point to mention some of the arguments used by those in favour of capital punishment, because they do not carry equal weight at all times. Sometimes one argument is put forward, sometimes another; sometimes one reason proves more convincing and sometimes another. But what is the use of reopening a controversy in which everyone knows in advance the arguments used by the other side and the replies that will be put forward? Despite all the evidence brought forward in numerous studies for its rejection, the example and value as a deterrent of the death penalty continues to be used by its supporters. Then there is the argument in favour of a selective death penalty—some say that only those who murder children should be put to death, others say that only those who murder old people should be punished by death and so on. There is a long list of those cases that deserve capital punishment—drug peddlers, those who seize hostages, dangerous drivers . . . When the list is complete, we can salve our consciences easily enough by concluding: 'Well, I would make an exception of those—I would apply the death penalty, although I am against it in principle'.

TWO PRESIDENTS OF THE FRENCH REPUBLIC

Neurosis based on insecurity, blindness, fear leading to a need for revenge and a general indifference—all these are contributory factors in the call for the death penalty. And, it has to be admitted, this call is often encouraged by the attitude of those in authority.

I have personally heard two successive Presidents of the French Republic express their views, in private, a few days before their election to the presidency, about the extreme responsibility imposed on the President as the only one empowered by the French constitution to grant a pardon to a prisoner condemned to death and the fear that they felt with regard to this solitary decision. Both emphasized their extreme hostility to capital punishment. 'I would pardon everyone', Georges Pompidou declared in 1969, 'And this might help public opinion, if the death penalty simply fell into disuse. The best way of risking a revival of passionate feelings would be to suggest that it should be abolished'. Five years later, Valéry Giscard d'Estaing made the same promise: 'There will be no capital punishment during my presidency'.

Georges Pompidou had, unfortunately, to give way on one occasion and place reasons of state first. He refused to pardon two men who, while serving a sentence of life for murder, had seized a warder as a hostage together with a woman social worker and killed them in the prison. One prisoner was condemned to death for murder, the other for complicity. The prison officers' trade union in France made it quite clear to the government that, if the first man at least was not executed, the prison staffs would conclude that their position was no longer safe. This threat brought immediate results and both men were sent to the guillotine.

Valéry Giscard d'Estaing also had to give way to public opinion and refuse to pardon the murderer of a child whose particularly horrible crime caused a wave of indignation. Since then, he has several times declared in public that he is opposed to the death penalty, adding on each occasion that the time has unfortunately not yet come and that people are not yet ready for its abolition.

Those in authority, then, even the most determined, give way and take no action. Several French ministers of justice were publicly in favour of the abolition of the death penalty before assuming office, but as soon as they were in office changed their minds, sometimes even going so far as to defend the use of the guillotine. This barbarous method of execution—but is there one that is not barbarous?—causes protestations from time to time. When this happens, deputies and senators do not suggest that this terrible appliance should be put in a museum department of mediaeval instruments of torture and never taken out again. On the contrary, it is seriously proposed that the method of imposing the death sentence should be replaced by an injection of instant poison.

LIFE IMPRISONMENT

If the arguments in favour of capital punishment are carefully examined, it becomes clear that there is one argument above all to which a satisfactory answer has, in France at least, not yet been found. This is the argument based on the fear that, if the murderer is not put to death, but condemned to life imprisonment, he will—after ten, fifteen or twenty years or longer, taking into account remissions and conditional release—eventually leave prison and kill again. It cannot be denied that that has sometimes happened, it is true. It is also true that so-called life imprisonment has never at any time or in any place been more than a long period of captivity.

What reply can be made to this argument? If we agree to let a twenty year old man go through the prison gates and not leave the prison until he dies—life imprisonment in the strict sense of the word—this would be to deny all possibility of redemption and to refuse to admit that he may change or improve. On the other hand, if we refuse to have strict life imprisonment, we would be placing an argument in the mouths of those who advocate capital punishment. It would certainly seem that several recent cases of the release of prisoners after a stay in prison and their killing again have contributed to a hardening of attitudes in France in favour of the death penalty. As long as this obstacle is not overcome, it would be foolish to hope for a strong movement in favour of abolition. We are therefore bound to conclude that our efforts should, in the present climate of opinion, be concentrated mainly on the question of strict life imprisonment. We should also recognize that the latter is impossible.

It is most important for those in power to guide rather than follow public opinion. By this, I mean all those in authority—not only politicians, who only too often concern themselves with legislation long after the change has already taken place in public opinion, but also and especially those with moral and religious authority, who tend fortunately to adopt a courageous attitude towards unpopular matters. (The French bishops' attitude at the beginning of 1978 is an example of this.) Even if it does not convince the majority of citizens, a firm attitude on the part of these authorities would give the political leaders the confidence that they need—moral certainty rather than the support of the electors—to overcome objections, put an end to the appeal in favour of the death penalty and to work in spite of resistance for an early abolition.

Translated by David Smith

Carlos-Josaphat Pinto de Oliveira

Violence in the Struggle Against Unjust Structures

REVOLUTION presents itself initially as an ethical enterprise. It starts with an appeal to the conscience of those that are oppressed. The actual conditions of the revolt are created by this conscientization which springs from the needs, the distress, the injustices, discriminations and the use of power publicly denounced by the leaders. Revolution draws its strength from the moral values which it wants to embody, establish or restore because it claims to be the force of right seeking to overcome the dominating violence in the shape of flagrant or disguised fraudulence. But this kind of strength soon turns into weakness. The discredit poured upon it from outside through international public opinion helps to increase the demoralization which sometimes paralyzes the partisans themselves. There is no doubt that this demobilizing because demoralizing crisis underlies the series of failures or half-successes which inevitably follow the first stages of revolutionary enthusiasm. But in all this I want to isolate and analyze here those factors which are ethical in the strict sense of the word.

It is obvious that revolution confronts people's consciences with unforeseen situations. It confronts them with border-cases, at first sight unsolvable, particularly when it is a matter of removing contradictions or liquidating internal or external opponents. These new ethical problems are faced initially from the angle of a pre-revolutionary conscience, a morality which prevailed in the cultures and societies before the liberation movement started. This morality continues to operate

93

among the peoples who judge the revolutionary process from outside. All thinking men and all men of action have met this kind of conflict: 'to keep your hands clean', 'not to have any hands at all' (Péguy), how to avoid making them dirty with violence or letting them shrivel up by doing nothing. Do such contradictions show up a particular kind of morality or an essential opposition between morality and revolution? I would like to concentrate on this basic issue of the relation between revolution and morality by tackling some of these cases of conscience which apparently run into deadlock.

WHAT DO THE BORDER-SITUATIONS TEACH US?

The border-situations and those cases of conscience which are at first sight unsolvable provide some precious indications. They show on the spot the trends and limitations of the ethical systems. The most typical situation, particularly for the European, is that of the resistance networks, of contacts in a country occupied by a victorious army and combed by its political police. Think of a dedicated leader who has taken it upon himself to liquidate two spies who would have put all the contacts of his network at risk. Being a Christian he first asks his parish priest for advice. His strict reaction is: 'No, you can't do that'. But after the 'execution' this same Christian, uncertain of himself or feeling guilty, goes to confession. The priest simply says: 'I understand'. He could hardly condemn the liquidation of those two dangerous opponents which, before, his morality would not allow him to accept.[1] And indeed, classical moral theology as taught in the (pre-conciliar) seminaries only allows killing in the case of legitimate defence or capital punishment. Both were no doubt excluded from the casuistic mentality of this good priest. Yet, the two Nazi spies, once taken prisoner, were no longer 'actual aggressors'. On the other hand, the resistance was not invested with that 'sovereign public authority' which, alone, could claim the prerogative to inflict capital punishment. Nevertheless, those brave Christians, challenged by an urgent decision in an exceptional situation, seem to have almost instinctively understood that they had to break through the throttling grip of such casuistry. Faced with the impossibility of detaining the spies in long-time imprisonment they saw that these spies, once back with the Gestapo, constituted a horrifying threat to the life of their own families and to the safety of the whole resistance network. In fact, faced with the local authorities' submissiveness to the occupying power and the impossibility of handing over the 'prisoners' to the military wing of the liberation movement, did this nucleus of combatants not represent that new democratic and juridical order which they were freely and voluntarily dedi-

cated to and which they initiated with their cool and rational behaviour? By accepting against their will the 'ultimate', and condemning
the two spies to death, they did so without cruelty, with the due personal respect of their opponents who were anaesthetized before being
executed. Did they not do what any honest man would do, obeying his
conscience in an unusual situation and rising above the cowardice, and
the theoretical hesitations which an ill-adjusted morality could not get
rid of? These questions become broader and inextricably complex in
the situation of young nations which, having become sensitive, perhaps
excited, by the sudden event of decolonization and their expectation of
justice, now pursue total liberation. For them justice must go hand-in-
hand with effectiveness, otherwise they would slip into merely nice
sentiments and get involved again in the morality which is objectively
linked with the oppression by the regime in power, honourably described as the established order.

Here is a story which I know of at first hand. A group of clergymen
wanted to meet a Latin-American revolutionary leader who was in fact
killed by the political police in 1968. They said they wanted to negotiate
the conditions for a possible participation by Christians in revolutionary activities while not wanting to dirty themselves by responsibility
for bloody violence. When they started to preach to him, the guerillero
felt stung in his honour, not to say his conscience, and broke into a
fierce but moving diatribe: 'Dear Fathers, do you believe that when I or
my men kill somebody we do it lightheartedly? Your teaching is the
right one to embarrass us before we act and to judge us after we have
done it. Tell me what to do. Give me men that are courageous, trained,
and committed unto death. We are sick of moral exhortation and de-
nunciation . . .' And this is the issue: in such border-situations, can
moral teaching rise above the level of exhortation and denuncia-
tion? Otherwise it will only echo outside the field of action and struggle.

BANKRUPTCY OF THE MORAL THEORIES

It seems to be extremely difficult to combine rectitude and effectiveness at the level of action and ethical consideration. It is the more
difficult as the undertaking of the revolution is complex and has taken a
long time to take shape. With all the things that go into the making of it
the revolution assumes the proportions of a world problem and conflict. Paul Tillich criticized the Encyclical *Pacem in Terris* for its op-
timism and stressed that the most tragic aspect of the human condition
is that it is impossible to fight for justice without committing injustices.
According to this theologian such weakness at the heart of power when

it wants to be at the service of love speaks volumes about the break between man's real essence and the conditions of his existence which beset individual and collective life.[2] It would be interesting to compile the typology of the various positions worked out by the theorists who have tried to overcome the contradictions which hamper or slow down the action. All these essays in ethical theory run into a dichotomy of real factors and ideal demands which they try to put into order or reduce. The most traditional classical formula distinguishes between the 'end' and the 'means'. The unarguably good objectives of peace, justice, equality, the triumph over discrimination, oppression and domination are characteristic of the revolution but are opposed to the methods of persuasion and force which it has to work with in order to make its liberating ideals effective. In fact, nobody could maintain that the end justifies the means. This maxim is commonly only used to decry the dealings indulged in by one's opponents. The most experienced men of action would hold with Gandhi that 'the end is in the means as the tree is in the seed'. And from a very different ideological angle, Leon Trotski's statement that there is an organic link between the means and the end which the revolution pursues,[3] is no less trenchant. Violence begets or perpetuates violence. The systematic use of lying, deceit and killing is in the long run bound to end up with discrediting and demoralizing the revolution. This conclusion is rooted in the very demands of effectiveness. It postulates, against Machiavellianism, that justice asserts itself universally and with overwhelming clarity throughout the whole revolutionary process. But it is in no way enough to dispose of the ambiguity of revolutionary practice and to get the consent of the supporters of social change. The proof of this lies in that, while Gandhi concluded from the necessary link between the goodness of the ends and that of the means to the exclusive recourse to non-violence, Trotski legitimized violence when serving the revolution because it then shared in the justice and goodness of the revolution. And, consistent with this notion, he labelled the 'virtues' of the *bourgeois* who obstructed the revolution of the proletariat as deceit and hypocrisy. Here the absolute dimension of moral goodness and the ultimate criterion for ethical assessment are simply passed on to history. History alone bears the teleological finality which legitimizes all the revolutionary objectives and methods. But since history, endowed with this finality, requires interpretation and depends on an analysis produced by the agents of the revolution, the actual multiplicity of these agents—infallible by right—creates a contradiction at the very heart of the revolutionary movement. Such a rise of totalitarian systems of Right or Left, all claiming the same criterion of the sense of history (expressed, as the occasion demands, by the slogans of 'national defence', the 'preservation' or the 'promotion of civilization'), finally shows the abstract, relative nature of such a principle. The non-violence (or better: the total dedication to the Truth) of the Hindu Mahatma compels man's conscience with a very different claim to absolute goodness. But by investing the (non-violent) means with absolute value does one not shy away from the changing imperatives of the situation, and, more radically, from the basic duty of enlightening a conscience that is alert to the objectives of a justice which demands recourse to other means? By what right can one posit *a priori* the axiom that violence cannot be controlled nor measured and apply this axiom deliberately when violence is the only means of breaking down a greater violence? The dichotomy of ends and means finds itself transposed into the 'principle of totality'. Here the social 'whole' faces the 'part' (individual or group) which it absorbs and subordinates to itself in a way which is analogous to that of subordinating the means to the end. The superiority of the whole then becomes absolute supremacy and the ultimate criterion where judgment is concerned. The part is subjected to the whole from which it derives its goodness and justification. It must be judged, and eventually punished, or even suppressed according to its submission and conformity or non-conformity to the 'good' which is embodied or intimated by the whole. History shows that there are three ways of applying this kind of doctrine. The first is that the whole and the parts are human subjects. Here it is a question of a society, a regime, a State composed of individuals, citizens. In this ethical perspective the social good, the common interest, becomes an absolute good and the ultimate criterion of assessing individual behaviour. Another view is to see the relation between the whole and the parts as a living organism within which the members are deemed to be at the service of the living whole in its totality. The evidence of certain injunctions (e.g., a gangrenous member must be cut out to save the life of the whole!) turns this organism-analogy into a major *locus ethicus,* a principle of arguing which is beyond criticism. Recently the principle of totality has been held to be applicable to a third line of argument. Moral life itself or one of its subdivisions is seen as a whole while the strictly specific activity is seen as a part of it. Every activity would therefore be in harmony with a whole moral set-up and its own moral qualification would wholly depend on this being related to the overriding quality of the world-wide set-up. The different formulations of the relationship between the whole and the parts are extremely vague and refer to a concept open to many interpretations. It could only play the part of a primary approach and would require the necessary precisions as derived from a precise definition of the whole, the parts, the various ways of integration, of participation and of the mutual interaction of various elements within the system to which they belong on the basis of some qualitative difference. Outside this studied consideration, incipiently set out by today's theories of the relevant system,[4] recourse to the analogy of the whole and the parts has become a source of *double-entendres*. Even the greatest masters have not been able to avoid this trap. The worst atrocities, the mutilation of prisoners and capital punishment itself have been justified by the glib appeal to this totalitarian principle.[5] Within these explanatory arrangements the revolution and the methods it adopts are set out as mutually dependent or independent according to the objectives or the process of the revolution, which are seen as a satisfactory or non-satisfactory principle by which the activities they instigate or the measures they inspire can be justified. Then there is another ethical model which is brought up, the one of what is 'directly or indirectly intended'. Here one considers the action itself, for instance, killing. In this case one tries to distinguish and scale the effects of the action and to judge them according to their rapport with regard to the deliberate intent from which they proceed and the way one effect may lead to another. This doctrinal procedure constitutes the properly ethical element which Christian thought has embodied in the theory of lawful defence as first formulated by the jurists. The moral foundation of this theory or of the attempts to justify morally certain kinds of violence—understood as 'defensive', responding to or parrying violence—is seen in the doctrine of the 'direct intent' to lie in the moral act as wholly dependent on what is deliberately intended, and the whole moral qualification of the act is derived from this precise point. In so far as it remains indifferent to the action and lacks the decision or efficacy to steer it towards the good, the 'good intention' is a barely disguised form of hypocrisy, magisterially exposed to ridicule by Pascal in his fifth *Lettre provinciale*. On the other hand, one can see some progress in this breaking up of the object of man's will. By looking at it in the light of differentiating the responsibility of intent (what is willed for its own sake, what is caused in a direct way, what is merely happening as a result, what is barely 'allowed' or accepted as an inevitable bad consequence in the pursuit of a necessary good or aim) room has been left for some solutions rightly applied to certain ethical problems. Thus, by the separated or combined recourse to the 'direct intent', the 'principle of totality', or the distinction between 'means and ends', a rather coherent moral system has been developed, covering respect for human life, social relationships aimed at bringing violence under control, and perhaps even a guarantee of peace. This system embraces the teaching on legitimate defence, 'capital punishment', the 'just war', 'revolt' as the ultimate weapon to get rid of a tyrant. In substantial agreement with the legal attitudes and the major needs of western society this kind of morality seems to have experienced a multiplicity of cases of conscience which slip through the solutions offered by its casuistry. Today it seems to have completely fallen apart and no longer able to impose itself as viable and practicable in the border-situations which have mushroomed under the impact of our technological civilization and the search for new types of society through evolutionary or revolutionary change. It also seems to fail through lack of a specifically Christian inspiration, particularly in the problems created by the proliferation of violence in the world. In order to relieve the strain on classical morality the generosity of leaders and prophets is turning towards a systematic recourse to non-violence.

Without pretending to offer here a critique of the various positions outlined above, I would like to expose the radical—and in my view incurable—failure of the ethical system which has inspired all these solutions. Its shortcomings point to its essentially inadequate nature. Action—particularly in its richest expression: political and revolutionary action—is beyond any moral system claiming to lay down norms (objectives) and their application to individual cases. Such a morality is reductionist because it is one-dimensional, and therefore lacks the complexity, the temporal nature, the continuity and lastly the achievement of the action. Only a pluri-dimensional system of ethics is capable of throwing light on decisions in the extreme situations created by action, particularly as embodied in the revolutionary process.

REVOLUTION AND A PLURI-DIMENSIONAL ETHIC

In order to meet this challenge one has to know how to integrate the valid elements of the theories mentioned above into an ethical project which is open to all the structural and dynamic aspects of the action and the revolutionary process and exposes the border-situations to the light of the ethical values understood in their original meaning, particularly when they are derived from inspiration by the gospel. These values—the truth to be communicated, human life, respect for the dignity of the person, the furthering of justice and the maintenance of peace—no doubt have an imperative absolute quality. But this quality cannot be translated into a code of 'dos' and 'don'ts' or, if one prefers, a corpus of 'objective norms', as a one-dimensional moral system would do. According to that sort of moral 'model' which is legalist or relativist in turn, these objective norms are declared to be unchangeable, inviolable and one is prepared to leave the decisions which these norms could neither authorize nor regulate to the individual conscience. The absolute character of the values in question is exacting in a different way. They certainly are a source which provides norms but also a source of dynamism, and of critical and creative inspiration. While the values guarantee the goodness of the norms in so far as these norms relate to the possibilities and requirements of the situation, they go beyond them in that they demand careful attention to be paid to the conditions of the action, and to necessary adjustments so that the norms do not wither away into ineffectiveness or get lost in the mutual conflicts or the demands of reality. These values therefore take on flesh and bones in the imprescriptible demands of universality, totality and premanence which must be implemented in history, both individually and collectively. This means that they demand to be applied according to the concrete possibilities afforded by whatever effective liberty one actually has at one's disposal and that one is committed to the opening up of new possibilities for freedom to serve the infinite demand of universality which characterizes these values. In any given situation this kind of demand tells us to do the possible, all that is possible and only what is possible today (e.g., to respect the value of life), whilst we commit ourselves to do better and more tomorrow, i.e., to extend the scope of liberty in view of the good, justice, and peace. Individual existence and the history of collective groups must therefore be seen and accepted clearly and courageously as a series of projects, brought about themselves by a series of actions. The appeal of the ideal and the imperative demands contained in the values must therefore make their influence felt simultaneously on both actions and projects but also on the interaction which constantly obtains between the one and the other.

Such a perspective makes it possible to integrate the moral theories about ends and means, the principle of totality, the indirect intent, and to overcome the kind of impasse in which action, particularly revolutionary action, gets bogged down.

Revolutionary action is undertaken as an element or 'part' of the liberating process. It can be seen as a means towards the establishment of justice and peace. And this is the overall and final aim which is pursued for itself and in itself (directly). But one cannot stay on the level of those moral teachings, which is the level of abstract generalities (the notion of 'ends and means' . . .). One has to tackle the analysis of the concrete ways in which action (the violent exploit) is related to the global project (the revolution, or a particular stage in its on-going process). Here are some samples of this analysis. Between the action and the project a process is at work, a process of mutual influence, of conditioning and perhaps modification which operates in a reciprocal way—I pointed it out above when referring to the diverging interpretations given by Gandhi and Trotski. And indeed the ambiguity can only be overcome when one considers that such interaction takes on a plurality of aspects: positive, negative, timely, progressive. The way they link up or separate will be decisive for the moral qualification of the revolutionary attitude.

Thus an act of violence committed in order to bring down or at least to weaken the opponents of the revolution may certainly have as its first result the elimination of obstacles to the situation of justice which the revolution aims at. But this positive result may have negative consequences corresponding to the effectiveness and the range of its effects. It can modify the course of the revolution in the direction of violence (violence stirs up violence), or push it towards a revengist attitude, spoil its sense of justice and compromise it in the eyes of the public inside or outside the movement. It is not difficult to see that these negative and positive results can influence the immediate, timely decisions or, to the contrary, lead to a progressive escalation of violence, but also lead progressively to a climate of understanding and possibly of coming to terms. The only action which is both effective and straight will be that which is inspired by justice and effectively aiming at peace. Then its influence will operate both in the sense of the positive orientation of the action and the restraint it will impose on the negative effects, i.e., deadly violence and hatred. Hatred is certainly effective, but only in a momentary and limited way. The hatred extolled by one or other famous revolutionary can only have this kind of restricted bearing. We may add that the ambiguity of the action will always remain a universal challenge. Non-violence, kind gestures, forgiveness are always liable to be interpreted as yielding to weakness and backing a whole unjust situation supported by other areas of omission, complicity, silence or insidious propaganda. The revolutionary process must strengthen the revolutionary consciousness, consolidate the partisans and the people in the ideals of the victory over the opponents. All this is true, but this triumph must be the triumph of peace, of moral values over tyranny, exploitation and the lust for power represented by the opponents. This kind of progress implies that in and through the action taken the agents and particularly the leaders of the revolution achieve a higher qualifying calibre and moral growth. Here the actual needs and situations make us turn again to the best attested ethical tradition, that of a moral doctrine of the virtues (Aristotle, Thomas Aquinas, Jankelevitch . . .). The technical, intellectual and moral qualification of the man of action is both required by, and the result of, action itself. At the start we said that revolution comes about as an ethical project. It really can only succeed by carrying this project to its fulfilment, by increasing the stature of all whom it enlists for its purpose. The revolutionary adventure is an outstanding and exceptional moment in history, and as such it will lead to the raising or the degradation of both the individual and the people. In the extension of the points outlined above I would like to concentrate more explicitly on the character and contents of a pluri-dimensional ethic which seems to be the only one capable of meeting the various challenges of the border-situations brought about by the revolution.

The dimensions here mean the specific aspects which are like so many salient points of the action that cannot be flattened out and demand an equally differentiated approach: intellectual, practical, involving critical alertness, adaptation to reality, the courage to modify it, and the constant practice of self-assessment. Let us take as the first dimension the content of an action seen in its essential structure and in the plurality of its immediate effects. A killing, a piece of deceit, or the taking of hostages are all actions with some inherent consistency which one can neither break up nor ignore. But neither can one stop at that because every action is situated and linked up with other elements in a project which has a temporal and collective aspect. The action is a unit within the private time consisting of the actual unfolding of each individual existence. But this same existence has its place within history, the time dimension consisting of events concerning mankind or one of its groupings. This personal and social historical condition of the action is inherent in it and invests it with a truly essential moral qualification. This qualification, derived from the insertion of the action into the history of the individual as well as history in general, assumes a twofold dimension. The first dimension is that linked with the actual situation.

The action will be good and adequate if it achieves the moral values—of justice, solidarity, truth . . . —with the right sense of how much is possible here and now. To live and act within the situation is by no means a concession or a compromise but rather conducting oneself in accordance with the real demands of the good which is already effectively possible. To cease today a spurious entente and to disturb an order based on injustice may be actually demanded by the search for to-morrow's peace.[6] The other dimension implied in the insertion of the action into the historical process relates to the prospect contained in the project for justice and peace which it brings about at least partially and in any case means to pave the way for. Action adopts the possibilities already present, tends to enlarge them and to create new ones. It anticipates the ideal which gave rise to the process of the just revolution and must motivate it. Certain gestures and even movements converge in the mission implied in this prophetic anticipation. This is shown, for instance, in the profound significance of non-violent movements, particularly when inspired by the gospel. They occupy a position of privilege in the world of just claims and in any genuine revolutionary process. Non-violence cannot be taken as an exclusive method, systematically rejecting any moderate recourse to violence. It is nevertheless meant to remind us of the ambiguity of any violent means which the actual situation may call for as the only effective way of breaking down the violence in power. There is no way in which the use of violence can remain animated by justice and lead to peace other than in so far as it is contained under the spell of universal solidarity. When that is the case, its use will not make it proliferate but will rather restrain it, and bring about some understanding, and a rational, peaceful dialogue.

EXECUTIONS IN THE NAME OF REVOLUTIONARY JUSTICE

I could not attempt here to give even the outline of this pluridimensional ethic but will try to show its relation to the most complex border-situations with regard to the exercise of revolutionary justice. From the start a revolution of liberation intends and has to inaugurate the future society which it proclaims and lays the foundations for. Whatever the geographical, historical and cultural peculiarities, this society must have the stuctures and government of a legal State which leaves increasing room for the exercise of freedom, respect for, and promotion of, the basic rights which all must enjoy. The revolution can only acquire authenticity and credibility through its effective fidelity to these moral values as shown in its factual behaviour. This kind of fidelity implies the practice of the ideals of the revolution as well as the effective defence of them in the neutralization of those who oppose the survival and the victory of the process of liberation. From the point of view of moral political behaviour this confronts us straightaway with the most fundamental right (and duty) although the subject of this right—the revolutionary movement—is still in the embryonic phase of its organization as a State. Indeed, from the point of view of the conditions of existence and the exercise of all human rights, the basic right is that expressed in art. 28 of the United Nations' *Universal Declaration of Human Rights:* 'Everyone is entitled to a social and international order in which the rights and freedoms set forth in this Declaration can be fully realized'. The moral legitimation of the revolution is tied up with this essential point. As a revolt it justifies itself initially on the basis that as a whole these basic rights are not ensured for all in society in a lasting way. It continues to justify itself in so far as it assures the people in the sectors and territories under its control that a new order which brings and promises justice is being inaugurated or at least is conducive to establishing such an order effectively. But since it no longer recognizes the justice and legitimacy of the old order, can the revolutionary movement claim authority for what is required to defend the new embryonic order, for the realities and promises which it heralds so that it can make revolutionary justice operative, including even capital punishment, in sentence and no doubt expeditious execution?

In order to clarify this problem we may begin by considering the demand for capital punishment as practised by certain groups, particularly by urban guerillas. When in the case of a kidnapping the ransom conditions have not been complied with, the kidnapping group declare that they have subjected their hostage to a 'popular' or 'revolutionary' trial, that the hostage has been 'condemned' and then 'executed'. This kind of judicial display is directed to public opinion, with its sense of morality and justice. In the end, this is linked with the common teaching on capital punishment, still prevailing among these revolutionaries or believed by them still to prevail in the society they want to do away with. But these subversive organizations are exactly and rightly reproached with availing themselves of a morality of which they themselves are far from fulfilling the conditions. On the other hand, a similar demand for capital punishment, presented as the prerogative of supreme power and practised with regard to great criminals as a deterrent, is today subjected to rigorous examination even by those who are involved in the defence of basic human rights. But while appealing to the people and denouncing numerous real injustices, the members of a terrorist network cannot really credibly claim to represent a definite people and a culturally and historically autonomous nation, to embody some sovereign authority, and to be a political power. How can one see in it, even in its embryonic state, a legal society, the beginning of a State based on the free and rationally informed consent of the citizens? In spite of accidental similarities this seems very different from the situation of resistance movements in militarily occupied countries or liberation movements of countries under an unjust or oppressive government. Particularly in the last case one can observe certain moral data which are of the utmost importance. They have made their weight felt when some Christian bodies have taken decisions with a view to aiding liberation movements in the third world. When an uprising is undertaken after mature reflection and preparation in order to liberate and advance a population whose support is sought and obtained as it gets better informed, then we have a movement which, at the level of social and political reality, is beginning to shape a legal State and is invested with a growing and effective authority. Its leaders have the responsibility, the right and the duty to defend the ideals and achievements of the revolution, and to protect the conquests and the destiny of their people. In the name of the legitimate defence of this common good and in order to secure that most fundamental right, stressed above when I quoted art. 28 of the *Universal Declaration of Human Rights,* the revolution will have to face opponents who are really dangerous and a threat. When in making justice function—no doubt in a precarious way, but that is the only way possible at that stage—the revolution sees in the application of capital punishment the only effective means of defending its task of bringing about justice and freedom, then it cannot renounce this measure without abandoning by the same token its aims and ideals. No doubt there will be the serious danger of yielding to feelings of revenge, of lapsing into settling accounts, and of stirring up the taste for violence among both the partisans and the adversaries. Here revolutionary realism will meet the demands of morality by trying to check such an escalation of violence. But more is necessary: following a morality which is heedful of all the dimensions of an undertaking as complex as a revolution, the leaders and partisans will be conscious of the absolute nature of human rights and will have to grant them even to their adversaries. No situation and no power could suppress fundamental rights such as the right to live. Even when the defence of goods and the most lofty values authorizes recourse to capital punishment the demand persists that interference with the right to live must be limited to the minimum and that the normal conditions exist which allow all to exercise their essential human rights. Particularly the right to live will not cease, even in the case of the criminal.

It would seem to me that the doctrine which justifies capital punishment on the grounds of the principle of totality is not well founded. This view holds that a man found gravely culpable has lost his right to live.[7] No authority is competent to pronounce that verdict and to deprive a human person of the opportunity to reform himself freely, even after the most serious misdeeds. But while, in saying this, I have rejected capital punishment as a normal statutory punitive measure in civilized and democratic societies, I maintain it as a last resort when it is the only means by which to preserve or secure the establishment or the exercise of the whole body of fundamental rights. This will no doubt be the case in revolutionary situations where the practice of justice creates the most thorny problems for the leaders, the partisans and the people that join them. There is no ethical system which, simply through its contents or its perfect consistency, can save one from the risks inherent in any personal decision. It should even avoid the illusion that it might ease the taking of decisions or of action when we are moving in the complex and changing realms created by revolutionary conditions and processes. Wisdom lies, on the contrary, in eliminating false evidence and ready-made solutions provided by doctrines worked out in some other historical context. What matters above all is to stir up people's conscience and to make them think about the moral demands implied in values and rights taken as a whole and their influence, about the historical or regional dimensions of the political problems, and about the actual conditions of existence in which individuals and peoples less fortunate than we are struggling along. The Christian presence and influence in revolutionary movements should never portend the imposition of a moral code which in all probability only made its mark in other conditions of life. Such a participation of believers is needed to ensure the need for lucidity, the courage to confront the perfection of love of the gospel with the problems, the worries and the hopes which the peoples and leaders of the new nations often experience in a wholly unusual way.

Translated by Theo Westow

Notes

1. The episode can be read in (Cel) Remy, *Aventures sur la ligne* (Lyon, 1974), pp. 217–53; for the actual quotation, see p. 232.

2. Cf. Paul Tillich's contribution to the collection *To live as men: an anatomy of peace,* published by the Centre for the Study of Democratic Institutions (Santa Barbara, California, 1965), pp. 13–23, with the quotation on p. 15.

3. See, e.g., L. Trotski, *Their morality and ours.*

4. I have alluded to this in my contribution to the Congres of ATEM, held in Fribourg (Switzerland), 19–22 Sept. 1978, the documents of which have been published in the *Suppl. de La Vie Spirituelle* (éd. du Cerf, Paris).

5. Thus St Thomas has only justified the actual position of mediaeval law on these points by referring to the principle of totality (*Summa Theol.* II–II, qu. 65, art. 1). The translator/commentator of the *Summa* for *La Revue des Jeunes* simply says: 'The article justifies mutilation from the penal and therapeutic point of view'.

6. These examples are taken almost word-for-word from the *Summa* II–II, qu. 37, art. 1, ad 2m.

7. This is the position of St Thomas (*Summa* II–II, qu. 64, art. 2–3), re-stated by Pius XII: 'The State does not have the individual's right to live within its power. . . . By his crime the condemned person . . . has already deprived himself of his right to live' (Alloc. of 13 Sept. 1952). I am taking this teaching further; for me the State is not competent even to pronounce on this (self) 'deprivation'.

Lelio Basso

The Problem of State Violence

THE problem of state violence as an instrument of punishment for those who violate its power or social order goes back to well-known ancient controversies, but I think the most important point in the discussion is the power shift in modern times: the centre of gravity of social life, authority and power has moved to the people, and become collective.

For as long as power was out of the hands of and superimposed on the people, who were mere subjects, crime aroused the vengeance of the offended prince, and the executioner, according to Joseph de Maistre, was the prince's instrument. Thus the prince was able to demonstrate his absolute power over the people. Any challenge to the sacred character of his power, any political crime was particularly heinous: *crimen majestatis* constituted sacrilege 'incompatible with the guarantees of normal procedure'.[1] Thus torture, which was normally banned for the *honestiores* and allowed only for inferior persons, the *humiliores,* was allowed to be used in political crimes also for the *clarissimi et perfectissimi:* in these cases *omnes torquentur.* This principle of classical law was perfected in medieval law, in which it retained the discrimination in the use of torture for common crimes,[2] the applicability of torture *erga omnes* was extended from the crime of treason to the crime of heresy, which was regarded as treason against God.

But with the rediscovery of 'man' during the long struggle of humanism and the renaissance, the eighteenth century clearly proclaimed the rights of 'man' against the absolute power of the sovereign.

And so, even the 'guilty party' is a human being and belongs to the human race and therefore at least one thing must be respected when he is punished: his 'humanity'.[3] It was no accident that Beccaria's essay 'On crimes and punishments' appeared only a few years before the Philadelphia Declaration of Rights and the French Revolution's.

With the institution of a democratic process, power, all power including the power to punish violations of the law, passed, at least in theory, to the people, and became collective. However society retained the power and the duty to punish, to impose respect for the common rules of life. But society must also give an example by respecting the 'humanity' of the guilty party: at the beginning of the bourgeois period the principle arose that the accused should be presumed innocent until he was found guilty,[4] that punishment should be human and concerned with the rehabilitation of the guilty party, and that these punishments should be controlled and limited by law. However the legal state, which should have guaranteed all this, and democracy, which should have represented the unity of people and power, of governed and governors, remained an ideal whose fulfilment was always denied by bitter reality. This seems obvious to a Marxist like me: how can it be possible in a society divided into classes, that the *humiliores* should enjoy the same rights as the *honestiores,* that the establishment, the functioning of society, and its laws, could be abandoned at the whim of democracy, empowered to upset everything simply by its vote? Of course universal and equal suffrage has been established nearly everywhere, but this happened after the setting up of a whole system of social mechanisms which conditioned human behaviour from birth to death. Of course Western democracies depend on the voters' consent, but this consent is the result of what Marx called 'the silent coercion of economic laws' and what we call today 'institutional violence'; school, indoctrination by the mass media, or ideological pressure of the system producing conformism.

This is the context in which I think we should regard the problem of the reversion to State violence, which is abandoning the humanization of punishments, the presumption of innocence until guilt is proved, respect for the humanity of those found guilty, even though these principles are laid down in all modern constitutions, post-war Declarations of Rights, and statements by the UN.

I think the reason for this is the crisis in contemporary society, which I regard as the most serious crisis ever to hit the western world. It is not just an economic crisis, the West has had many worse than the present one, but a crisis in the ideological system which is the foundation of consensus. People declared equal in theory have discovered the reality of their society founded upon inequality.

Especially in the underdeveloped countries, the awareness of human rights among the masses has grown faster than the capacity to satisfy their material needs and to ensure the functioning of the mechanisms of integration and consensus, partly because of the short-sightedness and conservative greed of the ruling classes and the rapacious selfishness of the multinationals. The old equilibrium based on the privileged few and the exploitation and suppression of the many has been endangered by the growth of democracy among the masses. A breach has been opened between the defence of the social order and respect for democratic values and the rights of man consecrated by constitution and law.

The example of Latin America shows how throughout a whole continent hundreds of millions of people can be deprived of the most basic human rights and subjected to arbitrary abuses whenever the social order feels threatened. In spite of the ancient tradition of coups and *caudillos* the dominant ideology of Latin American society was a mixture of Christian morality and democratic principles, both based on respect for human dignity. Some countries, such as Uruguay, were in fact a model of democracy in Western eyes. Now all these countries which belong to UNO have accepted its Charter, and the obligations it contains, including 'universal and effective respect for the rights of man and fundamental liberties for all, without distinction of race, sex, language or religion'. These rights were spelled out in the universal Declaration of 1948, whose introduction states that 'freedom, justice and peace in the world are founded upon the recognition of the dignity of the person and the equal and inalienable rights of all the members of the human family'. In the same spirit among the documents of the thirteenth General Assembly of Brazilian bishops we read that 'since God died for man, it is no longer possible for Christ's Church not to take man seriously, meaning people as they actually are . . . with their sufferings, aspirations and hopes'.[5] To justify the abandoning of these principles the so-called doctrine of national security was invoked, a doctrine supported by similar laws in the various Latin American countries. But it is ironical that this doctrine of national security, in the name of which democratic and Christian principles are grossly abused, claims to be defending these very same principles. According to their theorists and official statements, the world is divided into two blocs, the 'atheist and Communist' East, and the 'democratic and Christian' West, which are bound to come into conflict. This means that the citizen is required to give complete, total and indisputable obedience to his nation, in order to attain the permanent national goals proposed by the State to defend Western values. If the citizen does not obey, he must be forced to by any means available because national security is more important than anything else. Article 3 of the law on national security says that this comprises 'essentially the means destined to preserve external and internal security, including preservation from and repression of hostile psychological warfare. . . . Hostile psychological warfare is the use of propaganda and counter-propaganda and any activity on the political, economic, psycho-social, military plane whose aim is to influence or provoke opinions, emotions, attitudes, and behaviour of foreign, hostile, neutral or friendly groups contrary to the fulfilment of the National Goals'. And Article 45 defines subversive propaganda to be repressed by every means as 'the use of any means of social communication: newspapers, reviews, periodicals, books, bulletins, manifestoes, radio, television, cinema, theatre or anything else of that sort as vehicles of propaganda for hostile psychological warfare . . . political committees, meetings, processions and demonstrations . . . strikes are forbidden'. Clearly this means the prohibition of any expression of dissent: anything which is designated dangerous to national security is against the nation, its principles and order.

In order to understand what this law really means, we must remember that when it speaks of national security or national goals, it is not referring to the will of the people but to the will of the power held by a military clique which had violently grasped this power and imposed its dictatorship in order to defend this existing social order, that is to say the interests of the ruling classes of the country, and especially the imperialist interests of the multinational companies. And when it speaks of atheistic Communism to be destroyed as the chief enemy of national security, it means any progressive movement which tries to introduce any social reform to modify the existing social order or the internal balance of power. In Chile under Allende, Communists were also represented in the government, but in Brazil whence originated the wave of coups which then submerged the whole continent, and which was responsible for the doctrine of national security and its scientific application even to the lengths of torture and the boundless use of military power, President Goulart was miles away from the reality of Communism, and there were no Communists in power either in Uruguay or Bolivia. There was therefore no atheistic Communist threat even though the justification for the coup was that Goulart 'was preparing to Bolshevize the country' (Institutional Act no. 1); similar motivations were given for coups in other countries.

The chief result in Brazil and Chile, as also in Uruguay and Bolivia was the complete militarization of not only executive but legislative and judicial power,[6] and thus the end of rule of law. The citizen was restored to the condition of subject, and abandoned to the whim of the military: all citizens' rights were suspended. Anyone could be arrested simply on suspicion or for being a relation or friend of a suspected

person, and once arrested was completely at the mercy of inquisitors with unlimited power. The defence of the accused was no longer a public interest in the search for the truth but a mere formality which could be dispensed with. Witnesses for the defence might be refused a hearing, contact with lawyers became increasingly difficult,[7] lawyers were excluded from interrogations, especially because the police had the right to hold prisoners under indefinite arrest. Total isolation of the accused was the first grade of torture and could go on indefinitely, until it caused serious psychological damage. But isolation was merely a first step: the most savage and inhuman forms of torture, scientifically organized with the complicity of doctors as in Hitler's time, was a temptation to which irresponsible and totally uncontrolled policemen succumbed only too easily.[8] There were many cases of death or madness as a result of torture, but perhaps the most serious aspect was that the innocent man was subjected to the same processes and was never in a position to prove his innocence.

And what has happened in the West? Here too the crisis has shaken certain fundamental values upon which the system rests. And this has happened at the same time as the growth of technology and the increasing complexity of social life requires a perfect mechanism which cannot be allowed to break down. When Chancellor Erhard spoke of a 'formierte Gesellschaft' he put his finger on one of the fundamental characteristics of industrial society of our time, which must be a structured, organized and articulated society, well oiled in all its parts to be able to go on functioning in spite of its contradictions. But this requires the full consent of the people: if this is lacking, if the social mechanisms no longer produce it, then there is a risk that the whole machine will break down. In such a delicate and complex machine, the smallest fault, even a grain of sand, can cause disaster.

This is why total conformism becomes a necessity and dissent becomes the new crime of treason. Dissent hits at what is most sacred to society: the defence of the capitalist social order, the defence of property, profit and money which is the god of materialist Western society. And against this new form of treason state violence, within limits, is reinvoked. The principle of *omnes torquentur* is reborn.

In spite of the developments in democracy claimed to have taken place in various Western countries, the army, the police and the judiciary, have retained the character of 'separate bodies', they have never identified themselves with the people, or recognized the people's sovereignty, but have always considered themselves as legitimate holders of power, authority over the people. The army has remained a typical structure based on authority and hierarchy and discipline, not upon consensus, and thus completely undemocratic.

If during periods of democratic growth, social pressures also infuse democracy into the armed forces and make soldiers simply citizens in uniform, during periods of tension, when the mechanism of consensus fails, the defence of the social order reverts to principles of authority and obedience and the military spirit takes over from the democratic. Prisons have always been regulated on the model of military discipline, duly strengthened, which has often caused outbreaks of prison violence. During periods of democratic development, there were also reforms in prisons, inspired by the principles of the humanization of punishments and the re-education of prisoners. These 'modern' prisons co-existed with old-style prisons, which were overcrowded, unhygienic and incapable of reform. But new situations demanded, in Germany and elsewhere, the re-creation of special penal establishments.

Undoubtedly the Baader-Meinhof gang, like the RAF, like the Red Brigades in Italy, committed acts of terrorism, declaring war on society. In the face of this violence is state violence justified?

We answer no, as will be obvious from our previous remarks. If terrorism has become such a widely diffused phenomenon throughout the world, and in some countries, such as Italy, a mass phenomenon,[9] this means that it cannot be ascribed to the aberrations of sick minds but must have social causes. If, in spite of all the sophisticated psychological mechanisms of conformism, consensus is shown to be lacking in such a brutal way, clearly society itself must largely bear the responsibility and its first duty is to eliminate the causes. I cannot analyze these causes in every country: in Italy the causes are certainly failed reforms, grave social injustices and the scandal of the assured impunity for all crimes committed by the *honestiores*.

It may be said that a comparison cannot be made, because in Latin America democracy was attacked by the military, whereas in the West, parliamentary democracy remains, and still the Red Brigades or the RAF attack institutions and force the State to defend itself. But a democratic State should defend itself by democratic means: if it resorts to violent means, this opens the way to arbitrary violence and a state of law ceases to exist.

Of course the difference is enormous between the governments of Western Europe and Latin America but the principle is the same: the criminalization of dissent. The dissenter is considered as an enemy 'an enemy of the constitution', as he is called in Germany (this is not far from the Stalinist 'enemy of the people'), to be banned from his profession, condemned as a 'sympathizer' with terrorism [10] and if he commits a crime, 'he places himself, as a violent criminal, outside the rules of the game in our democratic State'.[11] And the 'democratic State' abandons the rules of democracy when dealing with such a person, and disregards the rights which respect every man because he is a human being. This reminds even an unbeliever like me of the teaching of Pope John XXIII who saw human faces everywhere, even in the wrongdoer, who still remains a human being after he has done wrong.

Translated by Dinah Livingstone

Notes

1. Alec Mellor *La Torture (Son histoire, son abolition, sa réaparition au XX siecle)* (Paris, 1949), p. 52ff.

2. In his codex in seven parts, Alfonso the Wise exempts *caballeros, hidalgos* and professors of law, and this is the general rule. On the other hand, it is rare to find a ruling like that of Louis IX's of France which exempts from torture *personas honestas ac bonae famae etiam si sint pauperes*. Cf. Lelio Basso, *La Tortura oggi in Italia* (Milan, 1953), pp. 58 and 60.

3. M. Foucault, *Sorvegliare e punire-nascita della prigione* (Turin, 1976), p. 80.

4. As in the United Kingdom.

5. 'Direitos humanos no Brasil hoje' in *Sedoc* (May, 1973), col. 1348.

6. *Tribunale Russell II—Brasile—Violazione dei diritti dell'uomo* (Milan, 1975) (referred to hereafter as *Brasile*), pp. 56ff. and *Cile, Bolivia, Uruguay: violazione dei diritti dell'uomo* (Venice, 1965) (referred to hereafter as *Cile*), pp. 27ff, 217ff. These two books contain the acts of the first session (Rome 1974) of the Russell II Tribunal on Latin America: the summary indications given here are amply documented.

7. *Cile,* pp. 81–82.

8. *Brasile,* pp. 202–3.

9. Of course the terrorists proper do not constitute a 'mass', but it is certain that they have widespread active support or simply passive approval, which continually furnish new recruits.

10. 'Anyone who continues to fraternize with the terrorists becomes their accomplice', said Chancellor Schmidt in the Bundestag on 13 March 1975.

11. Quoted by Chancellor Schmidt.

A. M. Ruiz-Mateos Jimenez De Tejada

Medical Care of Prisoners

THE ETHOS OF MEDICINE

'OF all those who devote themselves to the exploration of knowledge, the doctor is amongst the most responsible in the absolute sense of the word, because the struggle he undertakes is never finished. He must probe beyond the despair of those who have given up and beyond their fate. This is why he fights on all flanks with all the means of his knowledge in perpetual evolution'. This affirmation would seem to be absolutely right.

The '*ethos*' of the doctor springs from his humanitarian calling and therefore from his ethical or deontological convictions. The medical profession was one of the first to give a worthy expression to and to guarantee its '*ethos*' with promises, oaths and a medical code. The Hippocratic Oath is still in force after more than 2,400 years. Most faculties of medicine today use the Geneva Declaration approved by the World Association of Doctors in September 1948. Two of its commitments are worth singling out: (a) 'I will exercise my profession with conscientiousness and dignity'; (b) 'The health of my patient will by my first concern'.

Given this framework of medical professionalism, why is *Concilium* concerned to include medicine in an issue devoted to 'the death penalty and torture'? Is it a fact that medicine created for life can be using its immense scientific contribution to the knowledge of man in order to torture and kill?

THE FACTS CRY OUT

It is not possible here to give even a summary account of the protests coming in from all corners of the world against medical participation in various forms of torture of prisoners. All I can do is mention a few of the most significant if only by virtue of the debate their cases have aroused.

The atmosphere created in the last Congress of Psychiatry held from 28 August to 3 September 1977 in Honolulu was remarkable. From the beginning the psychiatrists—more than 4,000 of them—who came from all over the world, were involved in a campaign under the general motto of 'psychiatric repression against political dissidents in the USSR'; considered various sub-headings: (a) 'The abuse and use of Soviet psychiatry for political ends'; (b) 'A manual of psychiatry for dissidents', etc., . . . In the early sessions the information centre at the Sheraton Hotel provided extensive material on the use of mental medicine for political ends, especially in the Soviet Union, etc., . . .

It must be recognized that all the activities against the supposed abuses of psychiatry in Russia originated with the 'American Psychiatric Society'. This organization held a full session of free discussion in the great hall of the Sheraton Hotel on the subject of 'the ethics of the psychiatrist'. Once more the abuses of Russian psychiatry were condemned. By way of evidence, Dr Marina Welkhanskaya read out a long letter full of the most serious accusations.

Another well-known case was provided by the Russian psychiatrist Novikov. His declarations—made after his flight on 15 June 1977 on the occasion of the Psychiatric Congress in Helsinki on the subject of 'Suicide and preventive measures'—include an account of the pressures to which he was submitted by Prof. Georgil Wassiljewitsch Morosow, who is perhaps the most influential psychiatrist in the USSR.

A similar case is that of the dissident Vladimir Borisov who was arrested in Leningrad and interned in a psychiatric hospital for nine years.

The Soviet Union, however, is not alone in abusing medical and psychiatric methods. The 'Agency of Freedom of Information' has produced documentary evidence that from the end of the 50's till the 70's the C.I.A. engaged in a brainwashing campaign known by the code name 'Kutra' in which, besides the best agents of the organization, scientists—chemists, psychiatrists, hypnotists—also took part . . . X-rays, hypnosis, hallucinogens such as L.S.D. and other drugs were the order of the day in its proceedings.

'Great Britain found at least half guilty at the European Court of Human Rights for possible tortures and inhuman treatment in Ulster' (court proceedings between the Republic of Ireland and the United Kingdom). Five 'inhuman and degrading' procedures used by the British were enumerated: (a) Hooding of prisoners for several hours during interrogations; (b) Deprivation of sleep, food and drink; (c) Use of acoustics to confuse the detainee; (d) 'White noise' produced by electronic methods; (e) Prisoners forced to remain for a long time in painful positions: e.g., leaning against a wall with their arms out.

Dr J. A. Valtuena states: 'it is only in the last few years that medical intervention in the so called *intensive interrogations* carried out in the north of Ireland in the course of the operation of the English army against the I.R.A. has been established. The published documents (the Compton-Parker Report), each drawn up by three independent jurists summarize the processes of torture applied to detainees during interrogations'.

The reader must be sufficiently aware of what happens around the world for him not to be subjected to further examples. Just as a final note: Amnesty International puts the number of *political* prisoners throughout the world at more than one million, of whom most have been tortured in one way or another.

MEDICINE: TORTURERS AND TORTURE

The brute fact, given the present state of medical knowledge of human psychology, is this: 'we are all potential torturers'. Between 1960–1963 the 'Milgran' experiment made this perfectly clear. Even the mildest and most charitable of citizens could be turned into an obvious torturer when faced with the electrical apparatus constructed by Milgran.

Medical science with its achievements in understanding of neuro-physiology, neuro-surgery, psychology and psycho-pharmacology is in very grave danger of being manipulated for the purpose of carrying out the most refined forms of torture. It is better not to list particular applications of such knowledge for torture for fear that the information might be used by, or serve to stimulate, those who carry out such tortures. Techniques for breaking down personality through so called 'brainwashing' or 'mental rape' techniques are innumerable. Medicine realizes that any mind, however well structured or integrated, will in the end succumb to such techniques. The recent case of Aldo Moro is a vivid example of this. On the psychiatric level, one of the best studied cases is that of Patricia Hearst. The views of her psychiatrist, F. J. Hacker, present different levels of operation of her so called 'mental rape': identification with the aggressor; only those on the 'outside' are in the wrong; abject acceptance of the ideology of her torturers; etc., The extent to which professional practitioners of medicine have lent and are lending their knowledge to the ends of torture is unknown. Nevertheless, medical ethical conscience has been universally shaken by clear witness and perhaps even more by realizing its own capacity for techniques that only recently belonged to the realm of science fiction.

On the more positive side, I would like to give some examples of reactions by medical practitioners against any possible manipulation of their knowledge for the degradation represented by the phenomenon of torture.

MEDICAL CONSCIENCE AND TORTURE

In Spain we have for the first time held a scientific congress organized by the Spanish Society of Psychosomatic medicine and Psychotherapy to examine the subject of torture from a medical angle. This was held in Lérida from 29 October to 1 November 1977. The Congress fully adopted the declaration made by the World Medical Association at its Congress in Tokyo on 10 October 1975. This assembly defined torture as: 'the deliberate, systematic and excessive infliction of physical or mental suffering on the part of one or more persons acting either on their own or in obedience to orders from any type of power with the aim of forcing another person to give information, to confess, or for any other reason'. The first paragraph of the Declaration states: 'the doctor will not protect, tolerate or participate in the practice of torture or any other form of cruel, inhuman or degrading procedures whatever the crime. . . . The doctor will not provide instruments, substances or knowledge to facilitate the practice of torture. . . . The doctor will not be present on any occasion on which torture or other forms of cruel, inhuman and degrading treatment are either practised or threatened'.

This recalls the fifth article of the Universal Declaration on Human Rights of 1948: 'no-one will be submitted to torture nor to cruel, inhuman or degrading penalties or treatments'.

The Congress drew up a series of conclusions which the interested reader can find in the review *Psiquiatrika* 1/78, V.I, no. 1, Jan–Feb 1978, pp. 62–3.

With regard to *hunger strikes,* the Tokyo Declaration established that, although doctors could not force their practitioner to be fed artificially, they should look after him, relieve his sufferings and advise him on the possible consequences his attitude could have physically. The phenomenon of the hunger strike, in my view, poses serious problems for the medical profession. The doctor can appreciate that the hunger strike might be proceeding from evidently pathological grounds: clear processes of neurotic or psychotic regression. How far should a doctor respect this personal attitude when he knows that the subject is not acting from freedom but from a pathological situation which prevents him from employing the noble faculty of free will? In these cases medical prudence should use all the means in its power to help the sufferer abandon his strike and submit to appropriate treatment. In the ultimate instance of manifest alienation of the personality, he should act on the presumption of the consent of the sufferer. This at any rate is my view.

The UN asked the ONS to draw up in close collaboration with other competent bodies an outline of the principles of medical ethics applicable to protection of persons submitted to any form of detention or prison. Out of this came the two basic documents referring to medical-deontological problems: (a) The Geneva Declaration (or a modern version of the Hippocratic Oath) and (b) The Helsinki Declaration.

Another milestone in medical understanding of torture of detainees was the international symposium held in Athens which assembled a hundred medical professionals to discuss the theme of: 'violation of human rights: torture and the medical profession'.

Amnesty International in August 1975 included Spain amongst those countries accused of practising torture. The same organization has recently recognized that the situation there has improved.

The Medical College of Barcelona has recently raised its voice against torture and any possible medical participation in it. Nevertheless, the national conscience was revolted by the case of Agustín Rueda—a prisoner—who died on 13 March in the Carabanchel prison in Madrid, seemingly as a consequence of torture. The media implicated some medical practitioners at least on the grounds of passive co-operation. It is now in the hands of the Courts to establish the facts.

By way of conclusion, and without trying to evade the responsibility attaching to the medical practitioners of all classes with regard to torture and other procedures used against prisoners, I would like to make the following observation. Are we sufficiently aware of how far the institutions of certain countries can force the medical profession? We are conscientious and will take on responsibility for our own faults, but on behalf of many colleagues, I have to declare that their refusal to cooperate in torture frequently places them on the heroic plane. The heroic act, which is all that can be asked, invites understanding and compassion for many medical practitioners. Medical reflection on the subject is most welcome but let us not forget the reflection that should be made by institutions which place the doctor in this situation.

Translated by Paul Burns

PART IV

Documentation

Thomas G. Dailey

The Church's Position on the Death Penalty in Canada and the United States

IN THIS decade the Roman Catholic Church in Canada and the United States has voiced public opposition to capital punishment. This study will examine the official statements of not only the Roman Catholic Church but also those of other religious communities on both sides of the border.

CANADA

In 1973 the President of the Administrative Board of the Canadian Catholic Conference, Bishop William E. Power, in a statement to the Canadian Parliament stated in part:

> We consider it an illegitimate use of the Bible, especially the Old Testament, to quote texts in order to argue, in our time for the retention of the death penalty. Each biblical text supporting the death penalty must be studied in the light of its historical context, and not simply applied to present day Canada . . . In the New Testament Jesus . . . established the norm that violence and hostility are not corrected by countermeasures of violence and hostility . . . In our opinion, the case for retention of the death penalty has not been proven.[1]

Abolitionists would have preferred a stronger statement from the Canadian hierarchy. Yet, they welcomed the bishops' branding as illegitimate the ahistorical and uncritical application of the *Lex talionis* so often used by fundamentalist retentionists.

In 1976 the Administrative Board of the Canadian Catholic Conference again stated its opposition to the death penalty, with only one dissenting vote. The text of the declaration asserted that while 'capital punishment is acceptable only in a society which is not yet sufficiently well established to defend itself in any other way against those elements which would put in jeopardy the life of its citizens; this last is clearly not the case in Canada; . . . the spirit of the Gospel directs us towards forgiveness, clemency, and reconciliation. . . .' [2]

Bishop Emmett Carter, President of the Canadian Catholic Conference of Bishops in 1976 spoke in May of that year to a parliamentary panel on the abolition of the death penalty. He spoke in both French and English to underline the unity of both French and English speaking bishops on the issue. While conceding the right of the State to inflict the death penalty, he asserted that the question should be not one of right, but one of the better alternative. Suspension of the death penalty does not by itself cause an increase in criminal activity; this increase is due to many other causes of an economic, social and moral order, he noted. Bishop Carter also stated that in this matter one remains free in one's conscience. But, he pointed out, one should vote truly as one's judgment dictates not as political expedience indicates. [3]

Since capital punishment in Canada is legislatively a federal issue, the Catholic bishops have spoken on this question primarily at the national level through their Canadian Catholic Conference of Bishops.

Canadian bishops are known for a strong collegiality on vital issues and tend not to duplicate at the provincial level what has been promulgated on the national level. [4] Occasionally, however, statements are made such as that of Father Angus J. Macdougall, S.J., Executive Secretary of the Ontario Conference of Catholic Bishops. Father Macdougall, recalling that the Canadian bishops as a body had officially questioned the necessity of the death penalty as early as 1960, reaffirmed their 1973 and 1976 statements and cited their stress on the larger question of reform of the whole penitentiary system. [5]

On July 16, 1976, the Canadian Parliament abolished the death penalty completely. [6] No doubt the position of the Canadian bishops was a contributing factor. It must be noted, however, that there had been a strong call for abolition from other religious communities in Canada.

In a letter to members of Parliament in early 1976, the Canadian Council of Churches cited the Society of Friends in Canada, and the Mennonite Church in Canada, both of which have always opposed capital punishment; the United Church of Canada, which first called for abolition in 1956; and the firm opposition of the Anglican Church in

Canada, the Baptist Convention of Ontario and Quebec, the Salvation Army, the Lutheran Church in American-Canada Section, and the Presbyterian Church in Canada. The Canadian Council of Churches, which represents most of the religious communities in Canada, including the Catholic Church, spoke for all its member Churches at this time in condemning capital punishment.[7]

While the leadership of the Catholic Church and of the other Churches in Canada is virtually unanimous in opposition to capital punishment, public opinion polls in the seventies show the Canadian people increasingly in favor of its restoration.[8] If this trend continues, the death penalty question will surely become a political issue and reinstatement will be difficult to prevent. The Churches, therefore, still have hard work ahead of them if they hope to see capital punishment in Canada permanently abolished.

UNITED STATES

The National Conference of Catholic Bishops in 1974 stated the bishops' official opposition to the death penalty. Their complete statement on November 19, 1974, passed by a vote of 108 to 63 read: 'The US Catholic Conference goes on record in opposition to Capital Punishment'.[9]

While advocates of the death penalty saw this as a setback to their campaign, abolitionists saw in it little cause for rejoicing. They were disappointed not only by the brevity of the resolution, but more importantly, by the large number of bishops who voted against it.

The resolution, introduced by Bishop John May of Mobile, Alabama, passed after a seven-page document, prepared by a subcommittee of the Committee for Social Development and World Peace, was voted down. Much of the bishops' three hour debate on the rejected statement had centered on what several of them perceived as inadequacies in its arguments against the death penalty.[10]

Several State Catholic Conferences have issued official statements calling for the abolition of capital punishment: the Maryland Catholic Conference, the Michigan Catholic Conference, the Indiana Catholic Conference and the New York State Catholic Conference. (Each State Catholic Conference speaks on behalf of all the bishops in the respective state.)

Only one individual United States bishop has declared himself in favour of the death penalty. Archbishop Francis Furey of San Antonio stated in a lengthy article in the Archdiocesan newspaper: 'I am thoroughly convinced that people who commit heinous crimes, such as brutal murder and other crimes against society, should be made to pay with their most precious possession, their life'.[11] Archbishop Furey at this time also stated that the one-sentence statement, approved by the US Bishops in 1974, was not binding on the bishops. It was approved, he noted, as a US Catholic Conference statement which is not a 'juridical body'.[12]

However, at least 22 U.S. Bishops have made public statements in opposition to the death penalty. Many of these were resolutions signed jointly by leaders of other religious communities.

On 1 March 1978, the Committee on Social Development and World Peace of the US Catholic Conference issued a strong condemnation of capital punishment and added: 'We are deeply troubled by legislative efforts . . . to permit execution by lethal injection. . . . We find this practice unacceptable.'[13]

To the above Catholic Church statements calling for an end to the death penalty must be added an even longer list of declarations by other religious bodies in the United States condemning capital punishment in the past several years: The American Baptist Churches in 1977; the Church of the Brethren in 1957, 1959, and 1975; the Christian Church (Disciples of Christ) in 1957, 1962, and 1973; the Episcopal Church in 1968 and 1969; the American Friends Service Committee in 1976; the Friends Committee on National Legislation in 1977; the American Lutheran Church in 1972; the Mennonite Conference in 1951, 1961 and 1965; the National Council of Churches in 1968 and 1976; the Reformed Church in America in 1965; the United Church of Christ in 1969 and 1977; the United Methodist Church in 1976; the United Church of Christ in 1969 and 1977; the United Presbyterian Church in 1959 and 1977; the Unitarian Universalist Association in 1966 and 1974; the American Jewish Committee in 1972; the Synagogue Council of America in 1969, 1970 and 1971, and the Union of American Hebrew Congregations in 1959.[14]

Most Catholic Moral Theologians in the United States are opposed to the death penalty. Charles E. Curran holds that prudentially and historically it does not seem that capital punishment can be justified.[15] Jesuit theologian Richard McCormick, holds that the death penalty does not fit into contemporary theological awareness and Warren Reich of Georgetown University asserts that 'a Christian ethic based on the gospel and on a dynamic and developing view of human life finds it increasingly difficult, if not impossible, to justify the death penalty'.[16]

The Supreme Court of the United States in June, 1972, ruled that the death penalty as then imposed was a form of cruel and unusual punishment and therefore in violation of the Eighth and Fourteenth Amendments to the Constitution of the USX. In 1976, however, the Supreme Court upheld the discretionary death penalty statutes of three states. Since that time state legislatures have been actively reshaping their death penalty statutes to conform with the High Court rulings. Now thirty-two of the fifty states have capital punishment laws.[17].

Obviously state legislative efforts are a reflection of the pro-death penalty position of the voters. A 1978 survey shows 62% of the US public in favor of the death penalty for murderers, compared with 65% in 1976.[18]

Although this dip might be a small sign of hope that the efforts of the Churches and religious organizations are succeeding, it would be rash to be too optimistic. Much work still needs to be done. A stronger statement against the death penalty by a stronger majority of the National Conference of Catholic Bishops would be a most helpful witness to the gospel teaching on the inviolability of human life.

Notes

1. Canadian Catholic Conference, 90 Parent Ave., Ottawa, Press Release, January 26, 1973.

2. Ibid., March 4, 1976.

3. Ibid., May 26, 1976.

4. R. Drake Will, Assistant General Secretary (English) of the Canadian Catholic Conference, in *The Catholic Register*, Toronto, May 31, 1975, p. A2.

5. *The Sunday Sun*, Toronto, 4 April 1976, p. 33.

6. *Statutes of Canada*, Chapter 105, Ottawa.

7. The Canadian Council of Churches, 40 St Clair Ave. East, Toronto, Press Release, March 2, 1976.

8. *Gallup Report*, Gallup Poll of Canada, Canadian Institute of Public Opinion, Toronto, April 19, 1978: 68% of Canadians favour the return of a death penalty statute in Canada.

9. *Origins*, National Catholic News Service, 1312 Massachusetts Ave., N.W. Washington, D.C., Vol. 4, No. 24, Dec. 5, 1974, p. 373.

10. Ibid.

11. *Today's Catholic*, Archdiocesan Newspaper, January 28, 1977.

12. Archbishop Furey is correct. The National Conference of Catholic Bishops and the United States Catholic Conference are structurally distinct. The NCCB is the sponsoring organization of the USCC.

13. 'Capital Punishment: What the Religious Community Says', National Interreligious Task Force on Criminal Justice, Work Group on the Death Penalty (New York, N.Y., 1978), p. 7.

14. Ibid., pp. 5–37.

15. Charles E. Curran, 'Human Life', *Chicago Studies*, Vol. 13, No. 3 (Fall, 1974), p. 284.

16. Quoted in an interview in *National Catholic Reporter*, April 6, 1973, p. 21.

17. Nat. Interrel. Task Force, loc. cit., p. 3.

18. *Gallup Report*, U.S. Gallup Poll, American Institute of Public Opinion, Princeton, N.J., April 13, 1978.

Contributors

MOHAMMED ARKOUN was professor of Arabic and Islamic civilization at the University of Paris VIII and is now professor in the same field at the new Sorbonne. He has been visiting professor in Los Angeles and at Louvain-La-Neuve. He has published on Arab humanism, Islamic thought, and various aspects of Islam.

LELIO BASSO was in a concentration camp during the Fascist era in Italy. For many years he,has represented Milan in the Italian Parliament. He has published widely on the Italian Constitution, Rosa Luxemburg, neo-capitalism and the European Left and Marxism.

JAMES P. BRESNAHAN is associate professor of Christian and social ethics at the Jesuit School of Theology in Chicago and lecturer in medical ethics and human values at the Department of Medicine of Northwestern University Medical School. He has practised law.

FRANÇOIS COLCOMBET is a magistrate and has worked in various cities, including Lyons and Paris. He has held many honororary offices in the fields of human rights and French legal practice. He has published widely on legislation and justice.

FRANCESCO COMPAGNONI, O.P., is extraordinary professor of moral theology in the German seminar of the Theological Faculty of the University of Fribourg, Switzerland. He has published on Christian morality and fundamental morals.

THOMAS G. DAILEY is academic dean of St Augustine's Seminary and teaches moral theology in the Toronto School of Theology. He has published on the legitimate self-defence of a condemned person and on psychology and moral theological topics.

MARTIN HONECKER is professor of systematic theology and social ethics in Rome. He has published on the Church, canon law, social ethics, world responsibility, and associated topics. He is an Evangelical.

ALBERTO INIESTA is auxiliary bishop of Madrid and has taught in the Albacete major seminary. He has published on the fatherhood of God, and pastoral theology.

CARLOS-JOSAPHAT PINTO DE OLIVEIRA, O.P., is professor of moral theology at the University of Fribourg, Switzerland. He has published on the Gospel and social revolution, revolutionary theology, and moral choice in a technological civilization.

HERBERT RADTKE sells advertising. He is an honorary member of the Federal German Council of Amnesty International. He has published for Amnesty International.

ALFONSO MARIA RUIZ-MATEOS JIMENEZ DE TEJADA is professor at the Higher Institute of Moral Sciences of Madrid and extraordinary professor at the Complutensian University of Madrid. He is chairperson of a department of psychiatric and moral anthropology.

CLEMENS THOMA is professor of biblical science and Judaism at the Lucerne Theological Faculty, Switzerland. He is a consulting member of the Jewish religion commission of the Vatican Secretariat for Unity. He has published on Judaism and Christianity.

PIERRE VIANSSON-PONTÉ is a journalist. He is an editorial director of Le Monde and has been a local councillor since 1971. He is an associate professor in the political science unit of Sorbonne I University, Paris. He has published political historical studies.